THE BAFFLED PARENT'S
GUIDE TO
GREAT BASKETBALL
DRILLS

Jim Garland

Ragged Mountain Press/McGraw-Hill

Camden, Maine • New York • Chicago • San Francisco • Lisbon • London
Madrid • Mexico City • Milan • New Delhi • San Juan • Seoul • Singapore
Sydney • Toronto

796.323
GAR

To my sons Casey and Matthew

Ragged Mountain Press
A Division of The McGraw·Hill Companies

10 9 8 7 6 5 4 3 2 1

Library of Congress Cataloging-in-Publication Data
Garland, Jim.
   The baffled parent's guide to great basketball drills / Jim Garland.
      p.   cm —(The baffled parent's guides)
Includes index.
   ISBN 0-07-138141-4
   1. Basketball for children—Training. 2. Basketball for children—Coaching. I. Title. II. Series.
      GV886.25.G37 2001
      796.323′077—dc21   2001005235

Questions regarding the content of this book should be addressed to
Ragged Mountain Press
P.O. Box 220
Camden, ME 04843
www.raggedmountainpress.com

Questions regarding the ordering of this book should be addressed to
The McGraw-Hill Companies
Customer Service Department
P.O. Box 547
Blacklick, OH 43004
Retail customers: 1-800-262-4729
Bookstores: 1-800-722-4726

This book is printed on 70-pound Citation by Quebecor Printing, Fairfield, PA
Design by Carol Gillette
Production by Eugenie S. Delaney and Dan Kirchoff
Illustrations by Debra Heath
Photography by Mike Edge (Motion Concepts Sports Camps) unless otherwise noted
Edited by Jonathan Eaton, Margaret Cook, and Jane Curran

Contents

Players need to understand the process of play: collect, look, and make a decision. The second part, look, helps players recognize options.

Introduction

Great Basketball Drills was developed as a companion to *The Baffled Parent's Guide to Coaching Youth Basketball*, which has more background and details on the basics of coaching and basketball, or as a stand-alone book for coaches seeking the right tools to fix specific team weaknesses. If you're comfortable with the basics of the game, and just want more ideas for drills that will keep your kids involved and learning, *Great Basketball Drills* is all you'll need, so go for it!

Your new team will be made up of kids with different levels of ability and experience. Some kids will pick up skills easily, some will take more time. Some will be eager to learn, others will be nervous. Everyone, however, will want to enjoy their time on the team, and everyone can experience the thrill of individual and team improvement.

The Games Approach

Most of my teaching over the last thirty years has involved what is called the "games approach." Passing games like basketball require connecting passes with teammates and individual efforts to maneuver close enough to the opponent's goal to shoot. Teams that practice using small-sided drills that are fun, gamelike, and motivating will develop the skills necessary to prepare for the challenges of game situations. This is the games approach method.

Drills should provide players with opportunities for problem solving. Some drills included in this book are designed to find a way to keep possession of the ball, go toward a particular direction with the ball, or score. All of the drills will require the players to combine skills, concepts of play, and tactics to be successful. For variety, you can modify drills by changing the size of the playing area, number of players, number of balls, number of defenders, etc. If your players have a particular problem that's interfering with their game, check out the Troubleshooting Chart on pages 15–18. It will analyze what's causing the problem and then direct you to specific drills that will correct the problem.

The drills presented in this book are designed to give players lots of opportunities to develop individual skills and decision-making capabilities at each practice session. For example, many of the drills are confined to marked-off spaces, or *grids*. These grids are squares or rectangles denoted by markers at their corners, and their purpose is to restrict the amount of space players have for tactical decisions, forcing them to think quickly and act instinctively.

You'll find many opportunities to stop play and reinforce techniques and tactics previously introduced. Through observation these drills will also provide information about players' strengths and weaknesses that will be helpful in designing future practice sessions.

There is an increased likelihood of players' success if they are engaged in activities that are enjoyable, gamelike, and challenging. The

Make sure players have opportunities to ask questions and offer feedback.

games approach is not a substitute for skill mastery. Rather, skills are mastered during the small-sided game play. Individual instruction and demonstration will still be a part of the players' education. The players will be asked to take that skill knowledge and combine it with decision-making skills to be successful. The game is the teacher. The coach becomes the facilitator.

How to Use This Book

Great Basketball Drills is organized so that you can read it straight through, or you can go right to the section with the answers you need at that moment.

Chapters 1 and 2 introduce you to my coaching philosophy and give you the basics on coaching, including creating good relationships with parents, establishing a positive atmosphere, and building team spirit.

Chapters 3 through 9 have 125 step-by-step drills on all the fundamentals you need to improve your team's skills, including dribbling, passing, shooting, screening, and rebounding. The Troubleshooting Chart on pages 15–18 will help you pinpoint your team's problem areas and then direct you to appropriate drills.

Drills are assigned difficulty levels of "beginner," "intermediate," and "advanced." These can be thought of in terms of approximate age categories: beginner drills are generally for 6- to 8-year-olds, intermediate drills are for 9- to 10-year-olds, and the advanced drills are for 11- to 13-year-olds.

 beginner

 intermediate

 advanced

This book doesn't attempt to teach complicated schemes for breaking full-court pressure, elements of the fast break, or sophisticated offensive and defensive team strategies. The drills *will* help you teach the fundamentals of vision, communication, movement, and technique, providing a solid foundation of basketball skills that will stand your players in good stead as they play the game.

Summary

I hope the activities and suggestions in this book will be helpful. Be patient with their implementation. I've used this method of instruction for a very long time, and I know it works.

The players who have been exposed to this style of teaching program clearly demonstrate an understanding of

- how to play as a team player and not as an individual
- how to move efficiently with and without the ball
- how to make good decisions with the ball
- how to create and deny space efficiently
- how to execute basic fundamental skills of dribbling, passing, and shooting with proper technique

These are skills that result from a coaching style that promotes a decision-making, problem-solving approach to the game. Probably the greatest testament to whether or not this approach to basketball is successful is the fact that the kids I work with absolutely cannot wait to get to practice. They love it. They love it because instead of spending most of their practice time listening to me, they are having fun moving and learning while they move.

CHAPTER 1

Creating an Atmosphere of Good Habits

Promoting Teamwork and a Positive Environment

I was lucky—I grew up in a neighborhood with lots of kids, and one of our favorite sports was basketball. I still remember building our first backboard out of 2 by 4s, nailing an old rim on it, and standing back and admiring our work. We put plenty of nails in it so it wouldn't come apart. We had one small problem, however; we'd made our backboard so sturdy we could barely lift it off the ground, let alone hoist it ten feet in the air by ourselves. We had a dirt court with just enough rocks in it to challenge even the most skilled dribbler.

Not long after we'd established our undying interest in basketball, a much-improved venue became available. My friend Jay's father attached a rim and plywood backboard to his garage, which also had a 30- by 30-foot concrete playing area. We played there every day.

We played in a rec league, too, with practice twice a week and games on Saturday. I hated those practices. We stood in lines doing layup drills, making chest passes, shooting baskets—lines, lines, lines. I couldn't wait for practice to be over so we could go to Jay's house and have fun playing.

Things have changed a lot since then. I've coached high school basketball, directed basketball camps, and gotten a couple of degrees in physical education, but all these basketball experiences show me over and over that kids today want the same things that kids thirty years ago wanted. They want fun, gamelike activities with lots of action, and they need experiences in small-sided situations where they can have hundreds of touches on the ball, as well as time and space for decision making. This drill book is the answer: it emphasizes movement, technique, participation by all players—and involves far fewer lines!

Your most important job as coach is to create team unity and spirit. You'll have to take a group of kids with different needs, abilities, and interests and help them work cooperatively—blending their talents while understanding and appreciating them as individuals.

The best way to bring your team together is to foster a positive atmosphere. Your main goal as a coach is to provide a fun and rewarding basketball experience for your players. Kids naturally strive to do well, and they'll respond positively to encouragement. There's no one right coaching style, of course, but by using drills that involve lots of movement and touches on the ball, getting parents and kids enthusiastic about the team, and creating an atmosphere that's fun and supportive—not dictatorial—you and your team will be on the road to success. Promoting a positive environment means you and your players should respect the rights and property of others, have the courage to make mistakes, be honest with yourself and others, be responsible, and do the little things right. Have your players be responsible for their own equipment, water bottles, uniforms, and other duties as necessary.

Often, especially with beginning players, skills and concepts can be difficult to grasp. I found it was extremely important to let my players know it was OK to make mistakes while engaged in the learning process. Players will then feel comfortable stretching their potential and improving their skills. It's important to keep in mind that praise and encouragement work much better than yelling at your players or tearing them down. Of course, sometimes coaching involves criticism, but make your criticism constructive—and never let kids (or parents) criticize other kids.

Involving Parents and Players

Along with the varying abilities and needs of your players, you'll be dealing with the needs and interests of the parents. At the first team practice, it's a good idea to have the parents join your players for a short meeting before you start. Discuss the expectations you, the parents, and the players have for the team; this is an opportunity for you to reinforce what you expect from the players, such as good sportsmanship, being on time, and behaving appropriately during practices and games. Involve parents and players by asking them what they want from this experience and what they expect from you. Ask for feedback and suggestions from the parents about their expectations for the season, concerns about their children, and how they would like to participate. Remember, though, that as coach, you're the head of the team, and kids and parents need to respect that role.

My experience has shown that a coach is more successful using a more cooperative style and asking for parent and player input in determining these expectations. Probably the most important thing to remember is that both players and parents expect—and deserve—fair treatment. You should make it clear that you expect fairness—among players, between you and the players, and between you and the parents. This helps to foster a "we" atmosphere and begins to develop a bond of trust and mutual respect among parents, players, and the coach that is the cornerstone of a good relationship. The players will respond more positively in practices and games if they feel they are part of the process and not just doing what you've told them to do. The secret ingredient is the experience and genuine concern the coach brings to coaching.

In addition to team goals, you and your players should establish individual goals. More skilled players may have goals such as improving their 3-point shot or fast break. Other players may concentrate on more basic skills like effective dribbling and passing. That's where the drills come in. They are designed to work on specific areas, so whatever you and your players need to work on, you'll find drills to help. You'll also be able to develop goals for each practice and game and to use drills that involve all your players so no one is left standing around with nothing to do, and your kids are participating and learning all the time. During practice, you can adjust the goals and drills used as needed. Have post-practice reviews where you and the players discuss these goals, praising good performances and suggesting possible solutions for problems that occurred.

Improving Basic Skills

Think of the drills in this book as building blocks; as each player learns the basic skills and improves, the team as a whole will benefit. The players will learn to work as a cohesive unit, and that's what teamwork is all about. As you and your players learn together, you'll build trust, respect, and team spirit. The basics include mastering dribbling a ball with either hand, learning the difference between *open* (unoccupied) space and *closed* (occupied) space, and working as a team, not a group of "do-it-yourselfers."

One way to think about these skills is to divide them into two categories: physical ability and tactical judgment. Under physical ability are the actual skills of dribbling, passing, feinting, screening, defending, shooting, and rebounding. Tactical judgment is the ability of players to think on their feet and respond to the action around them. Here, players need to develop awareness of the space around them: Are they boxed in? Should they pass to another player? Are other players open? Should they pass long or short? Should they try for a basket? Do other players need help? Are they covering the right opponent? Tactical judgment, in other words, comprises the decision-making skills.

As players develop in ability and judgment, they'll garner a sense of personal achievement. Results will include better self-control, a good value structure, a higher awareness of the other players and thus an awareness of the team's welfare, and, ultimately, higher self-esteem.

When coaching high school basketball, my staff and I established three defensive and offensive goals for each game. Some of the offensive goals were scoring 14 points on fast-break opportunities, making more foul shots than the other team, and balancing shot selection from inside and out-side the 3-point area. Defensive goals included making more rebounds than the other team, limiting fast-break points to under 10, and letting the other team go to the foul line fewer than 15 times.

Just like after practices, have postgame discussions where you review the game. Don't emphasize winning or losing; instead, concentrate on the goals process you and your team have established. Did the team achieve its goals? What about the goals of individual players? What worked? What didn't work? Why? Get your players to use their problem-solving skills to think creatively. From this review, you and your players will be able to come up with new goals for the next practice and the next game. Make sure to praise all your players' efforts. The emphasis should always be on improving teamwork, improving players' skills, and having fun.

Winning and Losing

Some coaches feel that their role can be summed up in one word—winning. Regrettably, many parents, coaches, and players equate winning with success and losing with failure. It can be very difficult not to succumb to societal pressures about winning. Coaches who give in to the pressure to win will often be disrespectful to players, put all the best players on one team, give less experienced players less playing time than more experienced players, use ineligible players, and live and die with every call by the offi-cials. Having a winning team and a losing team in each game is a reality. The issue then becomes how winning and losing are perceived and empha-sized. Quite simply, being successful is winning, but winning may not lead to being successful. Being successful may be defined in many ways. Some would say that having the courage to participate and improving or showing progress are measures of success. I believe that you are successful if you accomplish the goals you establish with your team.

If you allow your team to think winning is their only goal, you'll set your team up for failure about 50 percent of the time. However, if you shift your emphasis from winning to accomplishing clearly defined goals during each practice and game, you'll teach your players to broaden their perspec-tives, learn about the game, improve their skills, and experience the fun and excitement of being a team. Remember that your players will take their cues from you, so give them good examples to follow. Emphasize that it's the overall experience that's important, not just winning individual games.

Organizing Practices

Practice Schedule

One of the first things you'll do as coach is create the practice (and game) schedule. A good rule of thumb is two practices and one game per week. Coming to practice less than twice a week can make it difficult for kids to learn and remember the skills they are working on, and more than this can create time-commitment problems for families of primary and middle school students. Have the schedule ready to hand out at the first practice so that every parent has a copy and knows what kind of commitment they're making to the team.

Productive Practices

The keys to productive and goal-oriented practices are keeping your players moving, giving them hundreds of touches on the ball, using drills to work on specific skills and situations, and maintaining a fun (but disciplined) environment. Remember when planning your practice that busy feet are happy feet. When players become bored, discipline problems become more frequent.

Probably what distinguishes good practice sessions from really good practice sessions are drills that teach creative problem-solving skills. Helping kids think creatively cannot be overemphasized. In game situations, players must rely on their creativity to be successful. Creative decisions must be spontaneous without coaching input and can only be accomplished if the players have a strong knowledge base to draw on.

It's important to remember that your players will have varying skills and will learn at different speeds. Make sure everyone understands the basics before teaching new skills. When your players are ready, gradually add new drills and concepts.

A good method of reinforcing a skill is to teach the same skill several different ways. For example, let's say you want to explain using the pivot. First, tell your players about the skill and then demonstrate it. Next, have your players practice the skill while you offer pointers. Then, the players continue to learn the skill during practice games.

Remember, each practice should include a variety of drills, activities, and small-sided and full-court games that will promote the development of individual and group skills, strategies, and concepts.

Keeping Kids' Attention

Over the years I've used several strategies to help keep kids' attention so that they have their best chance of learning. The first step is creating a culture for learning. The crucial element in creating this culture is the development of a "we" atmosphere that was discussed in chapter 1. Developing a "we" atmosphere establishes a standard where everyone, including the coach, is valued and respected. It is understood from the outset that everyone has a job. In some situations, particularly with older players, I have found it useful to have player contracts stating the role of the coach, parent, and player and to have everyone sign it as though it were an official document. This strategy helps to promote a culture of respect for others and to ensure that expectations are crystal-clear. One simple sign of respect that coaches can demonstrate early is to learn players' names quickly.

How practices are organized also affects a player's attention span. Coaches should be prepared by developing a practice plan (see Time Management, pages 13–14). The plan should provide for maximum movement while balancing small-sided activities, large-group games, and scrimmages. Players should not have long inactive periods standing in lines.

The plan should also have a method for bringing players together for instruction. I like using the huddle method when speaking to the entire group. I usually have the team sit down in a group. I sometimes sit with them but mostly stand in a position where I can see everyone. Making eye contact with everyone helps determine who is paying attention. If there is a particularly "active" player in your group who has difficulty staying focused or is distracted easily, you may want to make sure that each time you huddle with the team, you position yourself next to that player.

One of the biggest distractions is the ball itself. I use several methods for keeping the ball still when someone is talking, including having players sit with their legs crossed, with the ball in their lap and hands at their sides; having them sit with the ball between their feet; and leaving the balls on the floor while huddling in a different part of the court. As you might expect, huddling without the ball is the least distracting method.

Using starting and stopping signals to begin and end activities and to alert players when you want them to huddle is a good strategy. Some coaches use whistles, clap their hands, or raise their hands in the air to gain the attention of players. To help players value listening and huddling, make it a game. Tell them that during practice, for example, you will raise your hand when you want them to huddle with you. When you raise your hand, the first player to come and huddle receives a reward. Make the reward simple but worthwhile, like giving that player 5 minutes of extra shooting practice with you as a rebounder or being the first player to take a drink break.

When huddling with players, provide instruction that is brief and to the point. Prolonged discussions will cause players to lose focus. Make the point and keep them moving. Busy hands are happy hands.

Ten Commandments of Practice

I've developed the following list to help coaches plan practices. I call it the Ten Commandments of Practice.

1. **Maintain a safe environment.** Before each practice begins, make sure you check the court and remove any debris from the playing surface. When your players arrive, check that they have the proper footwear and that they've removed any jewelry, which could injure the player wearing the jewelry or another player. Players who wear glasses should have shatterproof lenses and head straps.

   Always carry a list of emergency phone numbers for your players, and know where the nearest phone is located. You should also have a first-aid kit, and you might want to take a first-aid course.

2. **Choose appropriate fitness activities.** Encourage all your players to have a medical fitness evaluation. In some situations, doctors will come to your facility and charge minimal fees for groups of players. In most cases, however, the players' private physicians will want to examine them. You should inform players and parents that any sport where there is physical contact and strenuous exercise has risks.

   Limit practice sessions for your youngest players (ages 6 to 8) to 60 minutes or less. For older players (ages 9 to 10) practices should run between 60 and 75 minutes. For your oldest players (ages 11 to 13), practices should be limited to between 1 and 2 hours. Remember to provide frequent water and bathroom breaks.

   Warm-ups and cool-downs are also a good idea. Include exercises that stretch the muscles gradually. I found that using a ball when stretching allowed more fun for players.

3. **Provide opportunities for hundreds of touches.** Use drills that let players have hundreds of touches on the ball. Encourage individual, small-group, and small-sided game activities to increase the opportunities for touches.

4. **Provide opportunities for creativity and problem solving.** Use drills that challenge your players. Keep them interested and involved.

5. **Provide opportunities for skill improvement.** Use drills that allow players to learn the same skills and concepts but at different levels, if necessary. Make sure all your players understand and are comfortable with the basics of a skill before moving on to more difficult variations.

    For example, let's say you're introducing a new dribbling move. First, explain the purpose of the new move and then demonstrate it so the players see what it looks like. Slowly run the players through the move until they have the basics down. Then have them use the skill in a no-pressure situation, such as dribbling as a group in a large *grid* (a square formed by game spots or markers), with game spots placed in it to represent defenders. *Game spots* are colored circles about 8 inches in diameter made of nonskid rubber; *game markers* are rubber cones, usually about 8 inches high. Both are used to define grid boundaries, and are available at sporting goods stores. Each time players come to a game spot, they must use their new skill to create a space and then move on to the next game spot. This type of activity will allow players the flexibility to work at their own speed.

    Next, have a defender stand on a line between two markers. The player with the ball must move the ball past the defender by using the new skill. The defender is limited to moving laterally and may not move forward or backward from the line. Make a game out of it if you like. Give the player with the ball 2 points if he can move the ball past the line without the defender touching the ball. Give the defender 1 point each time he touches the ball. Since you want to emphasize being successful with the new skill, award more points for the correct use of the new skill than the defensive effort. Play 5-point games, then switch positions.

    To increase the pressure, play the same game, but in a grid. Position the player with the ball at one side of the grid and the defender at the opposite side. When the player with the ball slaps it, the defender begins to defend. The defender earns 1 point if he touches the ball. The defender may move anywhere in the grid.

    When planning skill development sessions, you can use the skill development chart above as an organizer. I've used the dribbling drill discussed above as an example.

    Remember to be patient, and don't try to rush your players.

6. **Provide gamelike activities.** The more your team plays practice games, the better prepared they will be in actual game situations. Provide opportunities for your players to use the skills they have learned so far and get them to apply these skills creatively.

Skill Progression Chart—Dribbling

Skill Progression	Activity
1) Perform skill while stationary	1) Stationary Dribbling with game spots (drill 18)
2) Perform skill while moving under no defensive pressure	2) Partner Dribbling (drill 20)
3) Perform skill while moving under subtle defensive pressure	3) Jersey Tag Dribbling (drill 37)
4) Perform skill while moving under gamelike defensive pressure	4) One-on-One Dribbling (drill 35)

7. **Include small-sided games.** This is a must. Players love two-on-two and three-on-three games, which are great for developing endurance and providing opportunities for many touches. The best thing about them, though, is they make each player become totally involved. Players can't stand around and watch because of the constant changing of players. Variations, such as space, time, defensive pressure, number of players, and number and size of balls, will help teach many skills. The small-sided game should reflect the practice goal for the day. For example, if the goal is individual defense, then a one-on-one drill in grids might be appropriate.

When involved in partner or group work, make sure to vary how partners and small groups are divided. For example, for one activity have the players pick a partner; for another activity assign partners; in another activity divide the players by the color of their shirts or shoes. If you always allow kids to choose their own partners, they will tend to work only with their friends, or the best players will always want to work with each other. Players need to interact with all of the players on the team. Interaction will help to create understanding and tolerance of others.

8. **Provide lots of scoring opportunities.** All players want to score. There is nothing in the game of basketball that will bring a smile to the face of a player faster than scoring a basket, so try to provide lots of activities where lots of baskets can be scored. These can include shooting drills with no defenders, small-sided games with restrictions on types of shots allowed, such as off screen, screen and roll, layup, and the use of all baskets available.

9. **Have fun!** It's natural to want to continue doing something you have fun with. Try to make sure your players have fun by giving them lots of gamelike activities in practices, lots of touches on the ball, and

equal playing time during games. Above all, be sure you treat them — and they treat each other — with respect.

10. **Players should leave practice feeling good about themselves.** Everything else you do as a coach is meaningless if your players don't feel good about themselves. You can help build their self-esteem by having a sense of humor, evaluating their performance in relation to the goals you and the players have established, and developing a team relationship that is warm, respectful, and motivating.

Time Management

The best way I've found to manage practice time efficiently is to have a written outline for each practice. The worksheet on the next page will help you plan and organize the activities. Include a list of activities and drills in the order they will be practiced, the amount of time allocated for each activity, and any other notes you may have. You might also want to try using index cards for different phases of practice and keep them in a resource file for future reference.

Remember that this is just a sample. Activities and time allocations will vary according to the goals of each practice.

Take the time to review and evaluate your practice plan. Ask yourself a few simple questions:

- Does my plan have clear purposes and objectives?
- Is my plan reasonable?
- Is my plan relevant?
- Is my plan workable?

If the answers to these questions are all "yes," then you probably have a good plan. Remember to make sure your plan is age- and skill-appropriate.

When organizing your practice plan, remember that small-group activities offer you the flexibility of having different groups work on different skills. Or different groups can work on the same skill. The worksheet on the next page shows how you might organize a practice with four different stations.

Divide the players into four groups. The groups rotate around the stations, each working on a different skill.

Practice Session Worksheet (for 9- to 10-year-olds)

Team meeting (5 min.): _____
_____
_____

Warm-up/individual ballhandling in grid (5 min.): _____
_____

Stretching (10 min.): _____
_____

Station work (divide players into four groups; every 10 minutes, the groups rotate to the next station—players at station 4 go to station 1):

    Station 1: Shooting (10 min.): *Partner Layup*
_____

    Station 2: Dribbling (10 min.): *One-on-One Dribbling*
_____

    Break (5 min.) _____

    Station 3: Passing (10 min.): *Three-on-One*
_____ *Keep Away*

    Station 4: Rebounding (10 min.): *Partner Rebounding*
_____

    Break (5 min.) _____

Review team strategy of floor balance (5 min.): _____
_____

Full-court game (15 min.): _____
_____

Cool-down/review (10 min.): _____
_____
_____
_____
_____
_____
_____

Troubleshooting Chart

Use this chart as a quick way to find brief analyses of and suggested solutions for some of the common problems of young basketball players.

Problem	Analysis	Solution
Players swarm around the ball.	Occurs mostly with younger players who lack space and movement concepts.	Drills 1, 2, 5, and 8 address open, closed, personal, and general space. Drills 48–58 develop proper spacing and support.
Dribblers turn their backs on defenders.	Often players who lack confidence in their skills will fear having the ball stolen and consequently turn their backs.	Drills 3 and 4 improve visual scanning. Drills 7–9 and 14–17 develop understanding of changing speed and direction. Offer a variety of dribbling drills with no defensive pressure as in drills 19–24, subtle defensive pressure as in drills 24–34, and gamelike defensive pressure as in drills 35–45.
Players only move with the ball to the right side of the court when on offense.	Most players are right-handed and feel more comfortable moving the ball with their dominant hand.	Build confidence in using both hands. Develop ball-handling skills using both sides of the body. Include time in practice to explore using both sides as in drills 18–24. Add defensive pressure, subtle at first, as in drills 25–34, and more gamelike as in drills 35–45. Place restrictions on scrimmages (e.g., first pass must be made to the left side).
One player is a ball hog.	May be caused by not understanding how to share, particularly in very young players. Players may not understand the process of play: collect, look, and make a decision.	Try group discussion on teamwork and changing positions of players. Drills 57–63 develop the process of play. No dribble restrictions in scrimmages.
Players standing around during games without much movement.	Players have not been taught how to move without the ball.	Design practices that include opportunities to develop decision making and movement without the ball. Drills 1–17 will help players understand how to move. Drills 55–71 include lots of small-group passing drills. Drills 118–125 help develop screening techniques that enable a teammate to move with and without the ball.
Different groups of players need to work on different skills, but practices can be chaotic.	Players are different, with different strengths and weaknesses. Within each team, players will have varying individual needs for improvement, which should be addressed at practice.	Small-group drills provide the opportunity to work on more than one skill at a time. The use of grids helps to keep order by defining the space in which the players may work (e.g., one group works on a dribbling drill, another on a passing drill, and a third on a shooting drill).

(continued next page)

Troubleshooting Chart (continued)

Problem	Analysis	Solution
Players can't break full-court pressure.	Full-court defensive pressure is effective if offensive players don't communicate, don't stay within the process of play, are unable to execute dribbling and passing skills under pressure, and don't move to support positions.	Drills 48–53 develop communication skills through small-group grid work. Emphasize the process of play—collect, look, and make a decision—during all drills, scrimmages, and games. Drills 24–45 and drills 55–71 develop passing and dribbling techniques under defensive pressure. Drills 48–50, 57–63, and 66–71 develop support concepts.
Players have poor defensive skills.	Defense is often overshadowed by the need for players to score points.	Drills 94–110 instill a team attitude that values defense by keeping defensive statistics (e.g., deflected passes, steals, held-ball violations), setting team defensive goals before games, and providing small-group grid work to improve individual defense.
Players only want to scrimmage at practice.	Scrimmaging is fun and players often associate drills with less action and lots of standing around.	Use small-sided gamelike drills that provide hundreds of touches on the ball.
Players don't move fast enough to play player-to-player defense.	It's natural that some players move faster than others, but players can work on technique and teamwork.	Improve player reaction time with drills 94, 95, and 96. Improve their swing-step technique with drill 97. Provide lots of one-on-one defending opportunities with drills 98, 100, and 101. To protect slower players, use the help-and-recover tactics in drills 107 and 108.
Players lack the quickness to evade defenders.	Slower players need to rely on technique and help from teammates who are screening to create open space. When defenders have to make decisions instead of just concentrating on the player they are guarding, the offensive player has an advantage.	Improve players' swoop-and-go technique and attack the defender's front foot as in drills 87 and 88. Include development of solid screening techniques with drills 111–117.
Players dribble too much when passing would be a better choice.	There are five players on a team and only one ball, and beginning players often do not like to share. Intermediate and advanced players need to recognize that dribbling is used to create space for a pass, a shot, or penetration. Understanding the play process of collect, look, and make a decision will help players make good choices.	For beginning players, start with passing-only activities like drills 48–51, then move on to drills that combine dribbling and passing, like drills 52 and 53. Drills 57–63 work on passing without dribbling. Have some scrimmages where no dribbling is allowed.

Problem	Analysis	Solution
Players can't pass accurately.	Passing accurately requires communication, vision, and timing. Players need to be exposed to passing while under defensive pressure before they're pressured during games.	Work on passing from a stationary position to a stationary target with drills 46–48. Drills 49–54 work on passing to a moving player. Add subtle defensive pressure with drills 55–63 and gamelike defensive pressure with drills 64, 67, and 69–71.
Poor shot selection.	Knowing when and where to shoot is critical. Poor shot selection may involve bad decisions regarding range or defensive pressure. Too much emphasis on equating success with scoring points may also be a factor.	Use drills 79 and 81 to help determine players' ranges. To improve decision making, use drills 85 and 86 (subtle defensive pressure) and drills 87–93 (gamelike defensive pressure). Emphasize scoring goals for the team, not individuals.
Guards won't give forwards the ball on offense.	Guards typically control ball movement and sometimes believe they won't get the ball back if they pass it inside.	Include lots of opportunities for interaction between guards and forwards with drills 77, 83, and 89. Emphasize that spaces for outside shots by guards become more available when they pass the ball inside to a forward and then relocate for a return pass.
Players don't communicate with each other defensively.	This leads to confusion and scoring opportunities for the opposition. Develop communication during practices. Be sure to work on visual scanning techniques that allow players to see the action outside their own personal space.	Use drills 104–106, small-sided defensive drills with multiple players.
The opposition out-rebounds us every game.	Work on rebounding during practices. Rebounding involves instinct, technique, and desire. Even players that are smaller than average can be efficient rebounders.	Partner rebounding drills 118, 120, and 122 will help improve individual techniques. Drills 121, 123, and 124 incorporate multiple players and gamelike action. Use drill 125 to improve vertical jumping ability and timing. Emphasize rebounding during scrimmages by keeping score according to the number of rebounds instead of the number of baskets.
The team falls apart when the opposition plays player-to-player defense instead of zone.	Your team is not used to playing under pressure; practices likely don't involve enough decision making and defensive pressure. Players in zones defend spaces, so there are lots of opportunities to relieve defensive pressure by passing or dribbling away from the zone. Player-to-player defense requires more ball movement by teammates, and the only way to relieve defensive pressure is to create a space for dribbling or pass to a teammate.	Include lots of activities where players must create spaces for dribbling. Drills 25–34 provide subtle defensive pressure and drills 35–45 provide gamelike defensive pressure. Also include drills that promote moving without the ball; drills 56–61 and 63 provide subtle defensive pressure and drills 64 and 66–71 provide gamelike defensive pressure.

(continued next page)

Troubleshooting Chart (continued)

Problem	Analysis	Solution
We get as many shots as other teams but we don't score as much.	This may be caused by poor shot selection, poor shooting technique, or not practicing shooting with defensive pressure. Defensive pressure can cause a breakdown in technique.	Work on shooting technique with increasing amounts of defensive pressure from none (drills 72–84) to subtle (drills 85 and 86) to gamelike (drills 87–93).
My beginning basketball players have a hard time understanding screening.	Most 6- and 7-year-olds would rather hang to the ball than give it to their teammates.	These players are too young to understand screening. Spend your practice time on more basic skills.

Questions and Answers

Coaches often ask me for advice on how to solve problems they're having with their teams. Although the names and locations differ, the problems are similar.

Q. I have a team of 6- and 7-year-old first-year players who can't remember which basket they shoot at and which basket they defend. How can I help them?

A. For those of you who have never had the pleasure of working with this age group, don't laugh. This is a problem, believe me. Nets and scrimmage jerseys can be powerful tools in helping to establish order for this age group. Using two differently colored nets, one at each basket, will help players establish direction. The nets should be the same color as the scrimmage jerseys you intend to use, such as red and green. The players with red jerseys try to score at the red basket while the players wearing the green jerseys try to score at the basket with the green net. Players will instantly establish a sense of direction using these visual cues. If it's not possible to use differently colored nets, tie a scrimmage jersey to the bottom of the net or use a colored piece of tape on the backboard. Small pieces of colored tape positioned along the foul lanes appropriately (red in first block, green in second, etc.) will also help to reduce confusion during foul shots.

Q. I have a basketball team of 9- and 10-year-olds. How can I stop them from swarming around the ball?

A. This is a universal problem, particularly with younger players. I would begin the season by taking some time with the players to develop an understanding of space concepts. Drill 1, Open Space, drill 2, Closed Space, drill 5, Personal Space, and drill 8, Feinting, all found in chapter 3, address the concept of space and help players learn where to position themselves. It is important that players understand the ease with which they can maneuver in open space and the difficulties involved in dealing with closed spaces.

Then, I would use drills in practice that require decision making concerning space concepts. For example, if your players practice passing back and forth in two lines, you can't expect them to go on the court and understand how to pass efficiently with proper spacing and floor balance during game situations. Drills 48 through 58 in the Passing Drills chapter are designed to develop proper spacing and support concepts. The use of grids to help structure space and distances for connecting passes between players will help form off-the-ball movement habits that reduce the swarming effect. Emphasize that more open space will mean more time for decision making and fewer opponents to close spaces.

Q. We work on dribbling skills all the time. However, when my players are being defended in a scrimmage or game, all they do is turn their backs to the defender. How can I help them so they can dribble and see their teammates?

A. Your team may work on dribbling skills all the time, but it's *how* you work on these skills that's crucial. A player who turns his back constantly has a fear of having the ball taken away. For him to play with more confidence, challenging defenders, he needs to improve his vision and dribbling techniques. The first thing I would do is make sure the players understand how important it is to have good visual scanning techniques so they will know where defenders are located. These techniques are discussed in drill 3, Vision Tag and drill 4, Visual Dribbling. They should also know how to change speed and direction to create open space for dribbling. These concepts are addressed in drill 7, Avoiding Closed Spaces, drill 8, Feinting, drill 9, Herky Jerky, drill 14, Sideline Sliding, drill 15, Triangle Sliding, drill 16, One-on-One Jersey Capture, and drill 17, Large-Group Jersey Capture.

Second, players will develop solid dribbling techniques if they are offered opportunities to develop this skill through drill work on a regular basis, provided the drills are appropriately designed. Players should have lots of practice sessions that offer a variety of dribbling drills with no defensive pressure, subtle defensive pressure, and game-like defensive pressure. These drills should be structured so that players have the opportunity for hundreds of touches on the ball in a small-sided format. Dribbling drills that have no defensive pressure give players opportunities to explore, create, and refine dribbling techniques. Such activities are offered in drill 19, Dribble Pivot, drill 20, Partner Dribbling, drill 21, Follow the Leader, drill 22, Two-Ball Follow the Leader, drill 23, Sideline Dribbling, and drill 24, Imaginary Defender.

The next step is adding drills with subtle pressure, which require players to make decisions concerning how and where to move. If your players stand in lines dribbling across the floor and hand the ball to the next player in line, they have not been given the opportunity to integrate skill development and decision making. Drills 24 through 34 are designed for this purpose.

Gamelike dribbling drills offer the most competition and are offered in drills 35 through 45. Drill 35, One-on-One Dribbling is a great choice to help the dribbler who wants to turn his back on the defender. It is a small-sided one-on-one game played to 3 points. Basically, two players are in a grid, and the offensive player has to dribble the ball to another corner of the grid while being tightly defended. If she is successful without turning her back, she earns 1 point. If the defender creates a turnover or causes the dribbler to turn her back, the defender receives 2 points. Some time should be allowed for competitive drills of this nature at every practice. Turning their backs will mean no points earned and should help motivate players to be more inventive with creating space while dribbling. Once players form the habit of not turning their backs in the one-on-one game, they can transfer this habit to the five-on-five game.

Q. How can I stop my players from moving to the right side of the court every time our team is on offense?

A. It may be that the player who brings the ball up the court for your team has a best friend on that side of the court. If this is the case, change player positions frequently. I recommend this as a rule of thumb, particularly for younger players: Changing positions allows players to try different positions and decreases the possibilities of their being pigeonholed as a guard or forward. It also means all the players have the same opportunities to handle the ball.

However, I doubt if the problem is quite that simple. It is more likely a lack of confidence in dribbling with the nondominant hand. Most players are right-handed and feel more comfortable with the ball on the right side heading down the right side of the court. Building confidence in players' ability to use the left and right hands comfortably is a process that should begin with 6-year-olds and continue on up to high-school-age players. Spend lots of time at practices on drills for the nondominant hand. Do this using drills 18 through 24, which are designed to develop skills without putting players on display. Emphasize good visual habits while dribbling, including scanning. Maybe the player bringing the ball up court never looks to the left side. Add subtle defensive pressure as in drills 25 through 34 and more intense gamelike defensive pressure as offered in drills 35 through 45. Incorporating these dribbling drills in practice will help break the right-hand-only habit.

Coaches can also help their teams break the habit of only going to the right side of the court by modifying practice routines. One way is to put restrictions on scrimmages. Instead of a five-on-five scrimmage, you might have a three-on-three half-court scrimmage and restrict anyone from being on the right side of a line of game spots placed from the center circle to the middle of the end line under the basket until three passes are executed. You might then scrimmage five-on-five but instruct the players that the first three passes must be made on the left side of the line of spots. Another restriction might also have the players going to the left side for five possessions and the right side for five possessions, or even alternating sides on each possession with the first pass.

Q. How can I deal with a player who is a ball hog?

A. Some players are more individualistic than others. I truly believe bad habits are formed on the court because they are reinforced in practice. Although you may not intend to encourage ball hogging, you may inadvertently ignore the issue, which is the same as condoning it. On the other hand, you may want your best player doing most of the work for the sake of winning.

Sometimes the situation can be improved by an individual or group discussion concerning teamwork. In these discussions, let the other players express how they feel about not touching the ball in scrimmages and games. You may choose to change positions of players to help solve the problem. Instead of the player who is the ball hog being the point guard and bringing the ball up the court, select another player for that role.

It may be the case that a player who demonstrates what appears to be selfish play doesn't understand the process of play in passing games: collect—look—make a decision. Often beginning players will collect (catch) the ball and then put their heads down and begin to dribble to the basket. Usually this type of player will dribble into closed spaces and force a shot. The alternative is to insist that players demonstrate the second part of the process, which is "look," before they make a decision about what to do with the ball. This is an important aspect in building team play. Insisting that players look before deciding what to do next will slow their play down a bit and structure it more. It will give them visual cues to aid their decision making. In slowing down, they begin to think not only about themselves but about teammates as well. For example, they can see teammates moving to open spaces to receive passes. The process of collect—look—make a decision can be reinforced in small-group passing activities.

Use drills to develop this concept, beginning with subtle defensive pressure. There should be more offensive players than defensive players. One of the best drills to improve this process in beginning players is drill 57, Three-on-One Keep Away. In this drill, the passer must collect, look, and pass to a teammate who is in an open space instead of the one who is being defended. Drill 58, Double Movement Three-on-One, drill 59, Inside/Outside Three-on-One, drill 60, Team Keep Away, drill 61, Partner Direction, drill 62, Two-Circle Passing, and drill 63, Invasion, will also help develop this process. They are designed with increasing difficulty and require players to use other teammates to be successful.

You can also implement strategies in scrimmages to address individualistic play. During scrimmages, try restricting or eliminating dribbling, thereby forcing players to pass to each other. You might also try making a rule for particular drills that before a shot is taken, every player must touch the ball, a certain number of passes must be completed, the ball must be passed to each side of the court, or the ball must be passed to a *post player* (positioned in the 3-second lane) and *wing player* (positioned on the perimeter near an imaginary line extending from the foul line to the 3-point arc).

Q. When our team has the ball during games, my players seem to stand around looking at each other. How can I get them to move?

A. If they stand around in games, they probably stand around in practice. That may be because the practices are designed with activities where standing is the norm. Practices that have this look include long lines of layup drills, long lines of passing drills, and lines of some type of dribbling activity, usually a relay race (you may recall from the introduction that I find lines very dull, as do most players). Although skills are being developed to some degree, decision making is not incorporated; there is no thinking involved in standing in a line. Players cannot be expected to go into a game and demonstrate skills they have not had a chance to develop. Movement with and without the ball needs to be developed through practice drills.

Beginning players need time to develop how to move as provided in drills 1 through 17. After players have an understanding of how to move, they need to be challenged by adding defenders, with subtle pressure at first, then with greater, gamelike pressure. Their task then becomes not only how to move but where to move to create space for themselves or others. Adding lots of passing drills in small-group grid work, with subtle and gamelike defensive pressure, will help develop movement. Activities such as these may be found in drills 55 through 71. Drills to help someone else get the ball through screening techniques may be found in drills 118 through 125.

Q. Some of my players really need to work on dribbling, and some are great dribblers but need to work on passing. How can I organize a practice so that different groups of players can work on different skills without creating chaos or having kids standing around with nothing to do?

A. Try organizing your players in small groups, each working on a different skill. Using small-group drills and grids to restrict spaces allows you to give your players more individual attention and still involves all the players. You can rotate groups of players from grid to grid like station work or move on to an activity for the whole team.

Q. Whenever the opposing team presses us full-court, we fall apart. What can I do to prepare my team?

A. Basically, there are three types of full-court presses: player-to-player, zone, and combinations of the two. All are designed to create confusion. I recommend for all players 8 years old and younger that a no-press rule be implemented. They have enough trouble getting into their own half-court and creating scoring chances without being pressured in the back court.

For other players it is a matter of communicating with teammates, staying within the process of play (collect, look, make a decision), developing dribbling and passing skills that can be executed under pressure, and understanding and demonstrating movement to support positions.

Communication between players can be developed in small-group grid work, as in drill 48, Pass and Move, drill 49, Move to Support, drill 50, Group Pass and Move, drill 51, Diagonal Passing, drill 52, Circle Passing, and drill 53, Return to Passer. Use these drills to emphasize communication between players in all their drills and scrimmages, starting at the beginner level.

In breaking full-court pressure, vision is one of the most critical elements. Emphasizing the process of play where players must collect the ball and then look around before making a decision will prepare them for decision making against the defensive pressure. When they look around, they will establish where the defenders are located, how many defenders are creating pressure, and what kind of pressure it is—player-to-player, zone, half-court, full-court. Ball handlers also require information about where their teammates are positioned and where the open spaces are located. They can then make a decision as to how to attack the pressure.

Developing dribbling and passing techniques to handle pressure situations should be addressed in practice through small-group grid work with subtle and gamelike defensive pressure as indicated in drills 24 through 45 and drills 55 through 71. These types of drills were designed to incorporate decision making with skill acquisition.

Finally, players should understand that pressing teams cannot cover all the spaces on the court. Players without the ball need to recognize where the open spaces are, particularly against double-teaming zone presses, and move to a support position in those spaces. Most zone presses can be beaten with patience while getting the ball to the middle of the court and reversing it from side to side. Drills to help develop support concepts can be found in drills 48 through 50, drills 57 through 63, and drills 66 through 71. Players who understand how to move to support will find it easier to maintain spacing and floor balance.

Q. My team scores enough points to win most games, but we don't win because we play such poor defense. What can I do to correct this situation?

A. Athleticism, work rate, and technique are important factors in playing good defense. These factors alone will not guarantee that an individual or team will play good defense, however. Defense is an attitude that says "I won't let you beat me."

You can help instill this attitude in your players by emphasizing the value of defense in practices, scrimmages, and games. Very often players display the most effort and concentration in the beginning of practice sessions before fatigue is a factor. When planning practices, make sure to include defensive drill work at the beginning of practice sessions on a regular basis. Practices should include lots of small-group grid work to improve individual defense as found in drills 94 through 110. In these small-sided situations, players' weaknesses in executing various defensive techniques such as the slide and swing step can be observed and then corrected with small-group work. Players have the opportunities for hundreds of repetitions of fundamentals that may not be provided with large-group scrimmaging. Small-group situations are also the nuts and bolts of developing the "attitude." Many of these drills are designed to emphasize defensive effort, so more points are awarded when the defender is successful. You can bring out the competitiveness in your players by using these small-sided games where players may win by playing good defense. When players develop a mind-set that equates winning with playing good defense, defense is valued.

Another way coaches can develop a solid defensive attitude in their players is to assess defensive performance in drills, scrimmages, and games. Keeping a chart of who wins the defensive small-sided drills will increase the value of defense, especially if playing time in games is correlated with performing well in drills. Scrimmages and games can also be graded for defensive effort. For example, a player might earn 1 point for a steal, 2 points for a deflected pass, and 3 points for a held-ball (5-second count) violation. Place a point value on whatever part of the defensive effort is being emphasized, with the most points being awarded to this element. In the previous example, the held-ball violation is most desired, so it is awarded the most points. After grading each player, you can celebrate the defensive effort by naming a defensive player-of-the-game. You may even want to establish a team rule with the players that whomever is awarded the defen-sive player-of-the-game becomes the team captain for the next game.

Small-group work allows players to have lots of action. During small-group activities, coaches have many opportunities to stop the action and provide feedback.

Finally, you can help instill a defensive attitude by stating defensive goals before every game and by reviewing them at half-time and again at the end of the game. Limit the number of defen-sive game goals to three or four. An example of a team defensive goal might be to hold the opposing team to no more than 16 points from the 3-second lane.

Q. There are several people interested in helping with our team. How should I choose volunteers?

A. Wow! What a nice problem to have; usually coaches are scrambling to find help.

There are certain qualities I think you should look for in your volunteers. The most important one is to make sure they treat the players fairly. If they do, other considerations like availability, knowl-edge of rules, and playing experience can usually be worked out. Another quality to look for is their ability to communicate with play-ers and parents in a respectful manner. Finally, look for volunteers who have the same philosophy as you regarding winning and losing and the building of a positive atmosphere.

A good time to get some background on prospective volunteers is at the initial team meeting. Design a parent information form that includes questions on their interests, experience, availability, and special skills.

CHAPTER 3

Space and Movement Drills

All players need to understand the concepts of space (where to move) and movement (how to move). Beginning basketball players should initially concentrate on understanding open space, closed space, vision, direction, and speed so they'll be able to move safely and confidently.

Open space means recognizing, negotiating, and creating spaces without other players. *Closed space* means recognizing and avoiding occupied spaces to prevent colliding with other players, and denying space to other players—playing defense. Good *vision* means players should always be aware of the other players around them, keep their eyes on the ball, not the floor, and develop good scanning techniques (moving their heads from side to side) to increase their field of vision. Changes in *direction* and *speed* allow players to "create" or "deny" space to other players; in others words, playing good defense (denying space) and offense (creating space).

When introducing these concepts to beginning players, it's a good idea to start without a ball. Balls are very distracting, and players will tend to focus on the ball rather than the space or movement concept you're presenting. As your players improve, gradually add other factors such as speed and defensive pressure. You'll find that players who feel good about the way they move will tackle other skills with more confidence.

The drills on open and closed space come first because they deal with how players move safely. Development of good visual habits comes next. Good visual habits like scanning and breaking eye contact with the floor or ball will help improve your players' court vision and help them gather information about where their teammates and opponents are positioned and where the open and closed spaces are. This will enable them to make good decisions about what to do with and without the ball.

The final drills in this chapter involve changing speed and direction. Lateral movement in particular is emphasized because of its role in creating space offensively and denying space defensively.

Diagram key.

⌇⌇⌇⌇➤	dribble	**R**	red team player
- - - -➤	pass	**B**	blue team player
⟶	move	**Y**	yellow team player
⟋	screen	**N**	neutral player
X	defensive player	⬭	game spot
O	offensive player	⌂	game marker
C	coach		

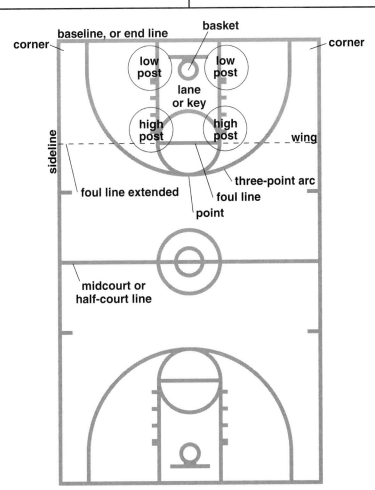

Court terminology.

1. Open Space

Purpose: To demonstrate how easily a player may travel, dribble, or pass through open space.	**Number of Players:** 1 (or 2) **Equipment:** 2 game spots, 1 basketball **Time:** 3 to 5 minutes

15 feet

1. Position two game spots so they are on a line on the gym floor about 15 feet apart.
2. Position Player O1 next to one of the game spots.
3. Player O1 moves from one game spot to the other.
4. Player O1 dribbles from one spot to the other.
5. Add a second Player O2 and ask Player O1 to bounce pass to Player O2.

At first this drill may seem unimportant, but it's the basis for teaching open space concepts. The crucial point is that players can move easily through spaces that are unoccupied. The term "open space" will be used often in coaching vocabulary. This drill will give players a visual reference to aid their understanding of this concept.

2. Closed Space

Purpose: To demonstrate how difficult it is to travel, dribble, or pass through closed space.

Number of Players: 3
Equipment: 2 game spots, 1 basketball
Time: 3 to 5 minutes

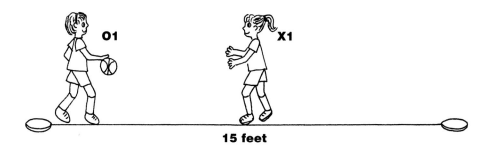

O1   **X1**

15 feet

1. Position the game spots so they are at each end of a line, 15 feet apart.
2. Position Player O1 near a game spot and Player X1 on the line halfway between the game spots.
3. Ask Player O1 if she can move along the line to the other game spot without touching Player X1.
4. Then ask Player O1 to try to dribble along the line to the opposite game spot without touching Player X1.
5. Position Player O2 on the game spot opposite from Player O1. Ask Player O1 if she can bounce a pass to Player O2 without bouncing the ball off of the line.

Player O1 has been asked to do the impossible. She can't move, dribble, or pass to the other game spot without the other players. You should ask her why. Player O1 will tell you that Player X1 is closing the space between her and the game spot she's trying to reach. Ask how Player O1 knew the space was closed. Player O1 will respond that she saw Player X1 there. This is the critical coaching point for beginning players. Compliment Player O1 for using good vision in recognizing the closed space. With or without the ball, players should move with their heads up while scanning. Point out to the players that when they see a closed space, they can change speed or direction to avoid it.

3. Vision Tag

Purpose: To develop techniques for visual scanning and breaking eye contact with the ground.	**Number of Players:** 12 **Equipment:** 4 game spots **Time:** 3 to 5 minutes

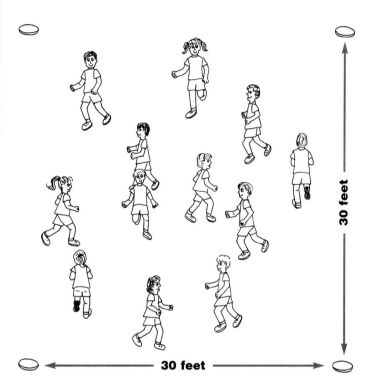

30 feet

30 feet

1. Position players in a 30- by 30-foot grid.
2. Players move freely about the grid in a vigorous manner.
3. As players move around, walk inside the grid and occasionally tag a player.
4. All the other players must call out the tagged player's name.

Players sometimes move with their eyes looking downward, which can lead to collisions with other players and possible injury. Encourage players to use good visual habits: scanning left and right and breaking eye contact with the floor. This drill encourages players to look up and see which player you tag.

4. Visual Dribbling

Purpose: To develop techniques for visual scanning and breaking eye contact with the ground.

Number of Players: 12
Equipment: 4 game spots, 12 basketballs
Time: 3 to 5 minutes

1. Position players in a 30- by 30-foot grid.
2. Players dribble the ball while they remain in a stationary position.
3. As they are dribbling, hold up any number of fingers.
4. Players call out how many fingers you raised.
5. Next, players move through the grid while dribbling.
6. Again, hold up any number of fingers.
7. Players again call out how many fingers you have raised.

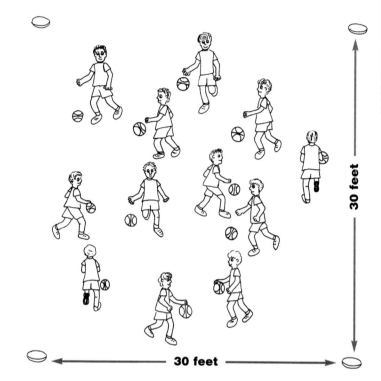

Encourage players to use good visual habits when in possession of the ball. The ball is a complication that affects vision for most beginning players because they feel they must look downward to control the dribble. If players start in a stationary position, they can practice good visual habits when in possession of the ball without fear of collision. Encourage those players who are not ready to break eye contact with the ball entirely to look up on every third or fourth touch when moving. This will help improve their vision and reduce collisions.

SPACE AND MOVEMENT DRILLS

5. Personal Space

Purpose: To develop an understanding of personal space and how it is affected by the movement of other players.

Number of Players: 12
Equipment: 6 game spots
Time: 3 to 5 minutes

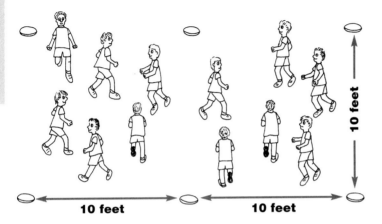

10 feet **10 feet** **10 feet**

1. Place two 10- by 10-foot grids next to each other so that they share one common side.
2. Position 6 players in each grid.
3. Players move about their grid, changing speed and direction without touching other players.
4. Then all of the players from one grid move into the other grid so that all 12 players are in one grid.
5. All 12 players try to move freely in the same grid.

As the players move initially, 6 in each grid, they will need to use good vision to avoid collisions (closed spaces) by changing speed and direction. This task should not be too difficult because each player has enough *personal space* (the space that immediately surrounds them) to permit this movement. When all players are in one grid, however, each player's personal space is reduced, demonstrating that the more players there are in a small space, the more difficult movement

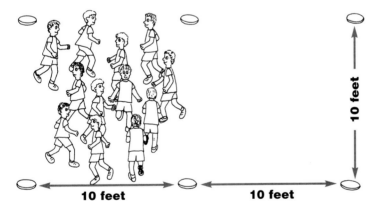

10 feet **10 feet** **10 feet**

becomes. This drill should improve players' understanding of personal space, help prevent clustering, and improve spacing in future activities and games.

6. General Space 👉

Purpose: To develop an understanding of player movement within general space.	**Number of Players:** 12 **Equipment:** 4 game spots **Time:** 3 to 5 minutes

1. Position four game spots to form a 10- by 10-foot grid.
2. Players try to move freely within the grid.
3. Reposition the game spots so they are 20 feet apart.
4. Again, players try to move freely in the grid.

This drill gives players a visual demonstration of how much easier it is to move when there is more open space. The added space gives them more time for decision making concerning direction and speed. This drill allows players to better utilize all of the spaces within the general playing space for better floor balance.

7. Avoiding Closed Spaces

Purpose: To develop good visual habits while changing speed and direction to avoid closed spaces.

Number of Players: 6
Equipment: 4 game spots
Time: 3 to 5 minutes

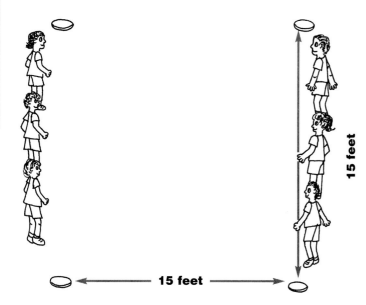

15 feet

15 feet

1. Position three players on each side of a 15- by 15-foot grid formed by using four game spots.
2. On your signal, players exchange places with the players opposite them by walking.
3. Next, players exchange places by jogging.

Encourage players to use good visual scanning techniques to determine where the closed spaces (other players) are located. As moving players detect closed spaces, they need to change speed and direction to avoid any collisions. The development of good visual habits will help create a safe playing environment.

8. Feinting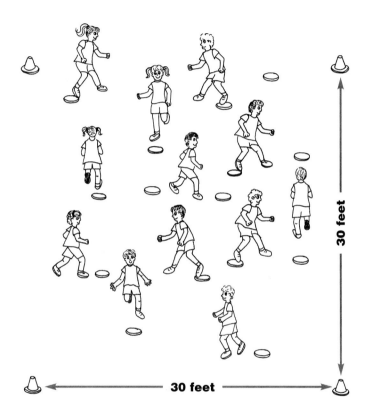

Purpose: To develop an understanding of how to change direction.

Number of Players: 12
Equipment: 4 game markers, 15 game spots
Time: 3 to 5 minutes

1. Randomly place 15 game spots in a 30- by 30-foot grid formed by four game markers.
2. On your signal, players start moving around the grid.
3. Each time they come to a game spot, they must change direction.

Changing direction is an essential movement concept to develop. This drill offers the opportunity to learn this concept with no defensive pressure. It will be the beginning stage for players to understand feinting, which is used to create space with and without the ball. Encourage players to change direction by flexing their leg, pushing off on the inside of the foot, and exaggerating the lateral movement. Players can incorporate other body parts in the movement, such as their head, shoulders, and hips.

30 feet

30 feet

9. Herky Jerky

Purpose: To develop an understanding of how changing speed can be used to create space.	**Number of Players:** 2 **Equipment:** 4 game spots **Time:** 3 to 5 minutes

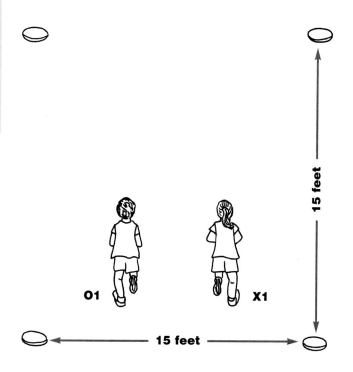

1. Position two players on the side of a 15- by 15-foot grid formed by using four game spots.
2. Player O1 stands beside Player X1.
3. Player O1 jogs to the opposite side of the grid, maintaining a constant speed while moving.
4. Player X1 jogs with Player O1, trying to maintain an arm's length distance from Player O1 as they jog.
5. Player O1 again jogs to the opposite side of the grid, this time changing speeds as she moves. Encourage Player O1 to accelerate quickly, and to slow down as she moves.
6. Players reverse roles.

This drill helps players understand that speed is an influence on space. As players learn to change speeds quickly, they can create more space between them and the players defending them.

10. Lateral Direction

Purpose: To develop an understanding of how to change speed and direction laterally.

Number of Players: 1
Equipment: 2 game spots
Time: 30 seconds

10 feet

1. Position two game spots so they are on a line about 10 feet apart.
2. On your signal, the player slides back and forth on the line and touches each game spot as many times as he can in 30 seconds.

Encourage players to flex their legs when starting and stopping and to move without crossing their feet. You can use this drill to assess player performance once a week.

SPACE AND MOVEMENT DRILLS

11. Creating Space

Purpose: To understand how changing speed and direction can be used to create space.	**Number of Players:** 2 **Equipment:** 4 game spots **Time:** 3 to 5 minutes

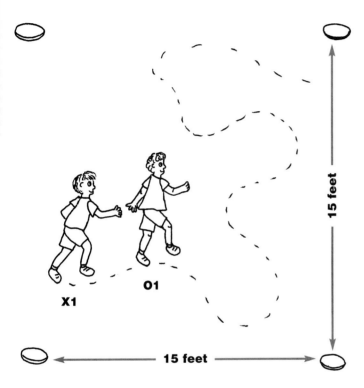

1. Position two players on the side of a 15- by 15-foot grid.
2. Player O1 stands one arm's length away from Player X1.
3. Player O1 moves to the opposite side of the grid.
4. Player X1 moves along with Player O1, staying one arm's length away.
5. Players repeat the action, but ask Player O1 to change speed and direction as he moves, reversing direction, accelerating, and slowing.
6. Player X1 tries to maintain the arm's length distance.
7. The players reverse roles and repeat the drill.

The defender, Player X1, will find it more difficult to maintain the arm's length distance when Player O1 changes speed and direction. This visual demonstration helps players understand that they can create more space between their defenders and them by changing speed and direction. A variation of this drill would have several partner combinations in the grid at the same time. Adding more players complicates the picture for beginning players because it affects their vision.

12. Jump Stop and Pivot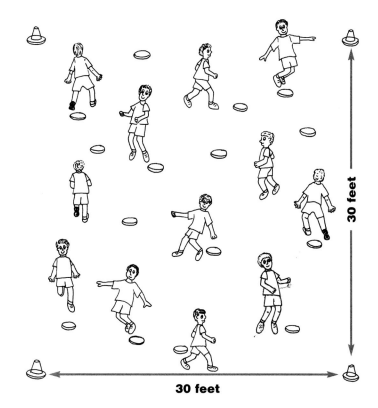

Purpose: To develop the proper techniques for the jump stop and pivot for changing speed and direction.

Number of Players: 12
Equipment: 4 game markers, 15 game spots
Time: 3 to 5 minutes

1. Randomly place 15 game spots in a 30- by 30-foot grid.
2. On your signal, the players travel through the grid.
3. Each time they come to a game spot, they jump over it, landing on both feet at the same time.
4. After landing, they reverse pivot and jump over the same game spot, landing on both feet again.
5. This time they pivot in a forward direction and move on to another game spot.

This drill demonstrates the value of the pivot in improving vision and creating space. Either foot may become the pivot foot.

30 feet

30 feet

13. Thirty-Second Lateral Movement

Purpose: To understand how to change speed and direction laterally.

Number of Players: 12
Equipment: 4 game markers, 20 game spots
Time: 30 seconds

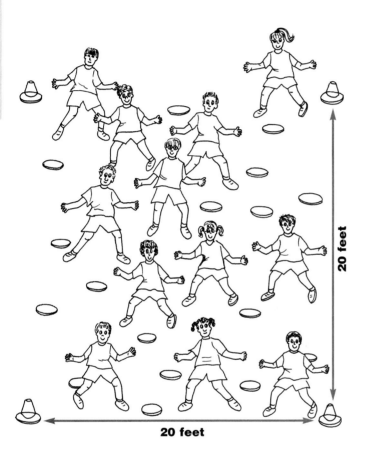

20 feet

20 feet

1. Randomly position 20 game spots in a 20- by 20-foot grid formed by four game markers.
2. Position players in the grid with legs flexed, feet shoulder width apart and in a sliding stance.
3. On your signal, the players slide and touch as many game spots as they can in 30 seconds.

The slide is one of the critical movement components in the game of basketball. Encourage players to flex their legs and to move their feet without crossing them. Use this drill as a weekly assessment, not to compare player performance with other players but to identify improved performance in each player. Having several players sliding in the grid at the same time will encourage the use of visual scanning techniques.

14. Sideline Sliding

Purpose: To develop lateral movement needed when executing defensive sliding techniques.	**Number of Players:** 12 **Equipment:** None **Time:** 1 to 2 minutes

1. Position players on the sideline of the court in a good defensive stance.
2. On your signal, the players slide to the opposite sideline, touch the line with their hand, and slide back.
3. This action is repeated for 1 minute.
4. Players count how many slides they were able to make in the 1-minute period.

Sliding speed and quickness are necessary components of individual defense. Do not allow players to sacrifice speed for good defensive techniques, however. Encourage players to maintain a low center of gravity with their hips, keep their heads up and their weight slightly forward, and slide their feet instead of crossing them. Players should keep their hands up at waist level and slightly extended, with palms facing an imaginary offensive player. Keep individual records of player progress without comparing one player to another.

15. Triangle Sliding

Purpose: To develop lateral movement needed when executing defensive sliding techniques.

Number of Players: 2
Equipment: 3 game spots
Time: 3 to 5 minutes

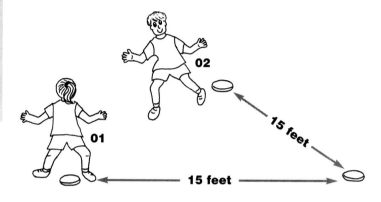

1. Position three game spots in a triangle formation 15 feet apart.
2. Player O1 and Player O2 each stand on one of the game spots.
3. Designate one of the players to be "it."
4. On your signal, "it" tries to tag the other player by using the slide step only.
5. Players must travel on a line from dot to dot.
6. Players reverse roles and repeat the action.

Encourage players to maintain good sliding techniques even though the complicating factor of speed has been added. Players should also be encouraged to use sliding steps when changing directions.

16. One-on-One Jersey Capture

Purpose: To develop an understanding of how changing speed and direction can create space while under defensive pressure.

Number of Players: 2
Equipment: 4 game spots, 2 jerseys
Time: 5 to 7 minutes

1. Position four game spots in a 15- by 15-foot grid, with players on opposite sides, facing one another.
2. Player O1 tucks two jerseys halfway into his shorts, one on each side by his hips.
3. On your signal, Player O1 tries to move to the opposite side of the grid.
4. Player X1 tries to stop Player O1 by grabbing one of the jerseys.
5. Whichever player is successful receives 1 point.
6. Players repeat the action until one of the players has earned 3 points and is declared winner.
7. Players reverse roles and play again.

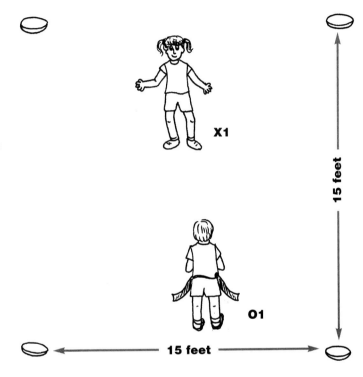

Encourage offensive players to change speed and direction explosively to create space. Quick lateral changes of direction and speed are beneficial in creating scoring opportunities.

SPACE AND MOVEMENT DRILLS

17. Large-Group Jersey Capture

Purpose: To understand how changing speed and direction can create space while under defensive pressure.

Number of Players: 12
Equipment: 4 game spots, 12 jerseys
Time: 5 to 7 minutes

20 feet

20 feet

1. Position 12 players in a 20- by 20-foot grid, all with a jersey tucked halfway into their shorts.
2. On your signal, players move through the grid, trying to grab as many jerseys as possible and to prevent their own jersey from being grabbed.
3. After one minute, stop the action, return the jerseys to players, and begin again.

Players may continue to try to capture other jerseys even after their own jerseys are captured. Encourage the use of good visual habits to avoid collisions. Players who quickly change direction and speed will be most successful in this drill.

CHAPTER 4

Dribbling Drills

Dribbling is a skill that basketball players of all ages love to use in practice and games. It is used to move the ball through open spaces when they are available. It is also used to relieve defensive pressure by creating open spaces for passing or shooting.

The dribbling drills in this chapter are fun, gamelike activities that provide technical and tactical challenges and opportunities to develop both the dominant and nondominant hand. You'll find many opportunities to introduce skill technique components such as bending at the waist with one foot slightly in front of the other (boxer stance), pushing down with the fingers instead of slapping the ball, using the correct force so the ball rebounds off the floor at a level between the knee and waist, and good visual habits. Learning to look up instead of down at the ball is difficult for beginners, so encourage them to look up on every third or fourth touch until their skills improve. Additionally, concepts of communication, vision, movement, change of direction, speed, and levels are reinforced through these activities.

The drills in this chapter, many of which are tag-type and small-sided activities, are presented in a developmentally appropriate progression from least difficult to most difficult. As the players become more proficient, complications are added to the drills, such as increased defensive pressure, reduced space in which to move, and additional balls. The amount of defensive pressure should be minimal for beginning players and increased as appropriate for advanced players. Each practice should include drills from this chapter that provide opportunities for combining dribbling with decision making. It is essential for players to know "how" to dribble, but it is just as important for them to know "where" and "when" dribbling is appropriate.

DRIBBLING DRILLS

18. Stationary Dribbling

Purpose: To develop basic dribbling techniques when stationary while under no defensive pressure.	**Number of Players:** 12 **Equipment:** 12 game spots, 12 basketballs **Time:** 5 to 7 minutes

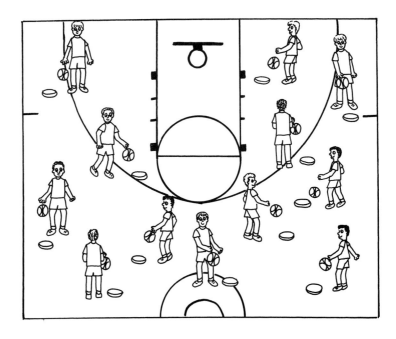

1. Position players, each with a basketball, in a scattered formation throughout the gym.
2. Place a game spot on the floor beside each player to identify their personal space.
3. Demonstrate correct dribbling techniques to the players.
4. Players repeat this technique by dribbling on their game spot.

It is critical for beginning players to have time to practice skills without the complications of speed, motion, and defenders. Instructing the players to dribble beside and over their game spots restricts their movement and defines their personal space. When basic dribbling efficiency is satisfactory, challenge them by requiring them to use the nondominant hand, crossover dribble, dribble between the legs and behind the back, and dribble figure eights. Encourage creativity in combining dribbling moves. As players' skills improve, add movement. Players might move around their game spots, go to a teammate's spot, and visit all of the blue spots while dribbling. Don't rush them into this movement phase.

19. Dribble Pivot

Purpose: To develop dribbling skills and pivot techniques while under no defensive pressure.

Number of Players: 12
Equipment: 4 game spots, 12 basketballs
Time: 5 to 7 minutes

1. Scatter players, each with a basketball, in a 20- by 20-foot grid.
2. On your first signal, the players begin dribbling through open spaces in the grid.
3. On your second signal, the players stop dribbling and pivot.
4. On your third signal, the players drop their ball, find someone else's ball, and repeat the procedure.

Encourage players to use a variety of dribbling moves and to dribble with their nondominant hand at least half of the time. Explain that the pivot will help them to balance as they scan and to protect the ball while being closely guarded.

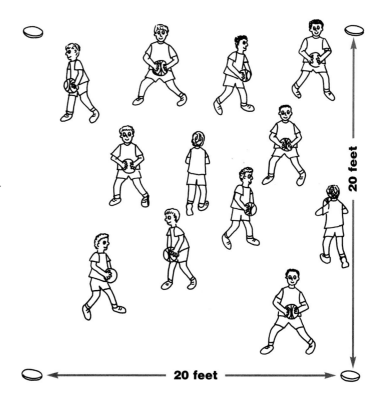

20. Partner Dribbling

Purpose: To develop dribbling skills while under no defensive pressure.

Number of Players: 12
Equipment: 6 basketballs
Time: 5 to 7 minutes

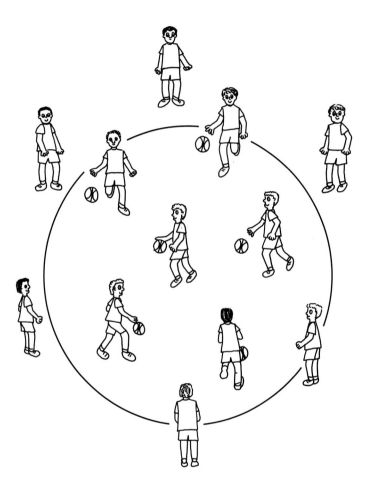

1. Position six sets of partners around a 20-foot diameter circle. (If there's no circle on your gym floor, use game spots or markers to make your own.) One player in each pair has a basketball.

2. On your signal, the player with the ball dribbles in the circle, changing direction and speed to avoid the other players while demonstrating a variety of dribbles that may be done in any order the player selects.

3. Dribbling moves are demonstrated for 1 minute. The partner with the ball then dribbles out to the partner on the circle, who repeats the dribbling action.

You may want to increase or decrease the size of the circle depending on player ability (the better the ability, the smaller the space should be). Players should be encouraged to use dribbles that are crossovers, spins, behind the back, or through the legs while maintaining good vision to avoid collisions. Players obtain visual cues from other players and are encouraged to show their own creativity.

21. Follow the Leader

Purpose: To develop dribbling skills while under no defensive pressure.

Number of Players: 12
Equipment: 4 game spots, 12 basketballs
Time: 5 to 7 minutes

1. Position players, each with a basketball, in three lines of four players in a 20- by 20-foot grid formed by four game spots.
2. Each player in line follows the first player through the grid while dribbling.
3. On your signal, the last player in line dribbles to the front of the line and becomes the new leader.
4. This action is repeated until each player has had the opportunity to lead.

   Encourage the leader to change direction and speed frequently. Good visual habits enable lines to move in open spaces.

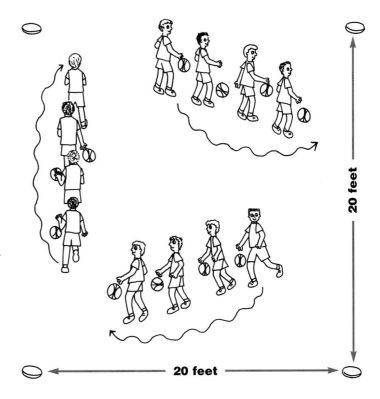

20 feet

20 feet

22. Two-Ball Follow the Leader

Purpose: To develop dribbling skills while under no defensive pressure.

Number of Players: 9
Equipment: 4 game spots, 18 balls
Time: 5 to 7 minutes

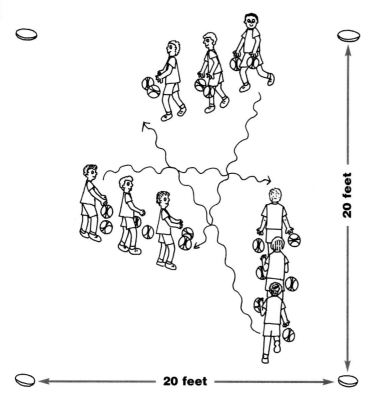

20 feet

20 feet

1. Position players in three lines of three players in a 20- by 20-foot grid formed by four game spots.
2. Each player has two basketballs.
3. The second and third players in each line follow the first player while dribbling two basketballs.
4. On your signal, the last player in line dribbles to the front of a different line.
5. This action is repeated until each player has had the opportunity to lead.

   It takes a lot of concentration to dribble two balls at the same time while moving through space. Encourage players to alternate the bouncing rhythm from simultaneous (bouncing both balls at the same time) to alternating (pushing one ball down as the other ball is coming up). If there are not enough basketballs available, only the leader dribbles two basketballs. As the new leader comes to the line, he is given a ball from the previous leader.

23. Sideline Dribbling

Purpose: To help develop dribbling speed while under no defensive pressure.	**Number of Players:** 12 **Equipment:** 12 basketballs **Time:** 3 to 5 minutes

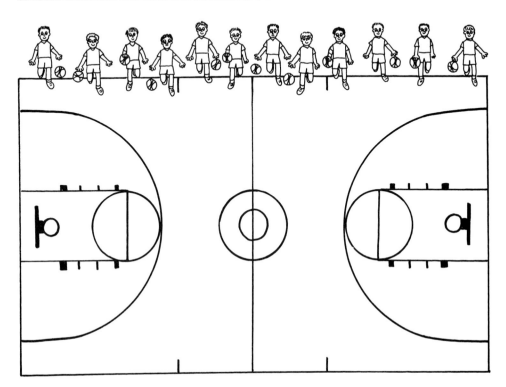

1. Position players on the sideline of the court.

2. On your signal, players dribble as fast as they can across the court, touch the other sideline, and return to their original position.

3. This action is repeated for 1 minute.

4. Players count the number of times they touch a sideline.

5. After players rest for 1 minute, the action is repeated.

For players to be able to dribble fast, they need opportunities to develop speed dribbling skills without defensive pressure. In this basic drill, players don't compare their dribbling skills to those of other players or don't feel they're on display because each player is too busy trying to reach as many sidelines as possible. Players can mentally record their number of touched sidelines and try to improve on this total as the season progresses. Players use their dominant hand when they are fresh. Once fatigue is a factor, insist that they use their nondominant hand for 1-minute durations, which will demand more concentration on their part to be successful.

24. Imaginary Defender

Purpose: To help develop dribbling penetration skills while under no defensive pressure.

Number of Players: 12
Equipment: 3 game spots for each basket, 12 basketballs
Time: 3 to 5 minutes

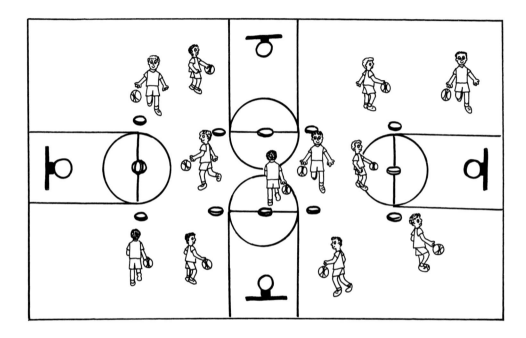

1. Scatter players on the court.
2. At each basket place one game spot on the middle of the foul line and one to the right and left of the foul line extended.
3. On your signal, the players dribble randomly to whichever basket they choose.
4. As they dribble toward the basket, they will encounter one of the game spots, which serves as an imaginary defender.
5. Players must use a "dribble move," such as a crossover or spin, before finishing their shot.
6. They continue on to the next basket of their choice, and when they encounter another game spot, they are to use a different dribble move.

When using any shooting drill with 6- and 7-year-olds, lower the basket to a height of 8 feet to reduce the amount of mechanical errors in the shot process. As the intermediate players are approaching the game spots (defenders), encourage them to combine feinting using the head, shoulders, and hips with the dribble move. Also, encourage them to encounter game spots in different locations so they are shooting at the baskets from different angles.

25. Speed Dribbling with Defenders

Purpose: To help develop dribbling speed while under subtle defensive pressure.

Number of Players: 12
Equipment: 18 basketballs
Time: 3 to 5 minutes

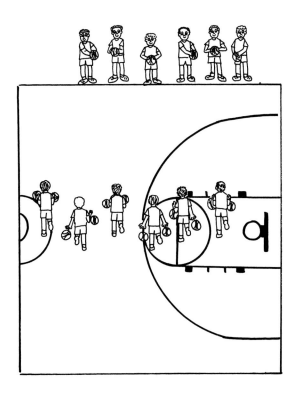

1. Position six offensive players, each with a basketball, on the sideline of one half-court.
2. Scatter six defensive players, each with two basketballs, on one half-court.
3. On your signal, the offensive players have 2 minutes to see how many times they can dribble as fast as they can from one sideline to the other. They receive 1 point for each successful attempt.
4. If any of the defenders, who must dribble two basketballs at a time, can tag an offensive player, that player must subtract 1 point from her score, go to the closest sideline, and begin again.
5. After 2 minutes, players reverse roles.
6. The player with the most points wins.

Encourage players to dribble as fast as they can through open spaces. Good visual habits will help them to avoid closed spaces. Vary this activity by allowing offensive players to use only the nondominant hand.

DRIBBLING DRILLS

26. Circle Dribbling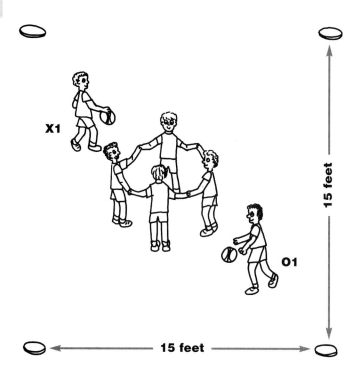

Purpose: To create open space using the dribble while under subtle defensive pressure.

Number of Players: 6
Equipment: 4 game spots, 2 basketballs
Time: 8 to 10 minutes

X1

15 feet

15 feet

O1

1. Position four game spots to form a 15- by 15-foot grid.
2. Four players stand in the middle of the grid and hold hands.
3. The other two players, each with a basketball, stand outside of the circle on opposite sides.
4. Player X1 is designated "it" and must try to tag Player O1.
5. On your signal, Player X1 dribbles toward Player O1, going around or through the circle of players. Player O1 also dribbles a ball but may not go through the circle.
6. After 1 minute, or if Player O1 is tagged, players change roles.
7. If Player O1 loses control of the ball, Player X1 wins.

Encourage Player X1 to change direction and speed faster than Player O1 in order to get close enough to tag him. Looking up when dribbling helps players determine when these changes should occur. Encourage players when changing direction to dribble the ball from one hand to the other (that is, when moving from right to left, they should change from the right hand to the left hand). Beginners often change directions but keep the ball in the same hand.

27. Crazy Critters 👉

Purpose: To use change of speed and direction to move through and create open space while under subtle defensive pressure.

Number of Players: 12 to 15
Equipment: 4 game spots, 12 to 15 basketballs
Time: 8 to 10 minutes

1. Use four game spots to make a 10- by 10-foot "guardhouse" in the middle of one half-court.
2. Designate three players as guards. They are the "crazy critters" and won't dribble a basketball when they move.
3. All other players must dribble when they move.
4. On your signal, players move through the half-court, avoiding the crazy critters if possible.
5. If a player is caught by a crazy critter, she must go to the guardhouse.
6. This player may be rescued from the guardhouse if one of the players on the outside makes a bounce pass to her and she uses a bounce pass to return the ball.
7. The game ends if all players are in the guardhouse.

There are countless opportunities in the game to stop the action and reinforce open and closed space tactics. The concepts of vision, communication, and movement are also intertwined.

28. Team Triangle Dribbling

Purpose: To develop change of speed and direction when dribbling while under subtle defensive pressure.

Number of Players: 13
Equipment: 4 game spots, 3 basketballs
Time: 8 to 10 minutes

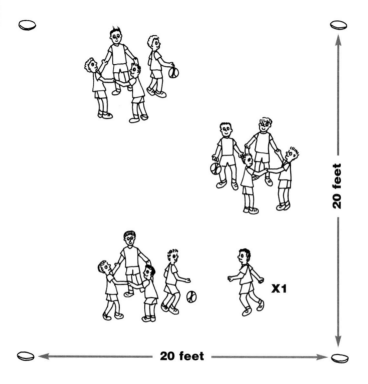

20 feet

20 feet

X1

1. Position three teams in a 20-by 20-foot grid formed by four game spots. The three players on a team form a triangle, and the fourth player stands outside the triangle with a ball.
2. Designate one player not on any of the teams to be a defender, Player X1.
3. On your signal, Player X1 tries to tag one of the dribblers.
4. The triangle of team members moves as a group to try to protect their dribbler.
5. If their dribbler is tagged, they must all sit down.
6. The winner is the team whose dribbler is not tagged.

Encourage players in the triangle to stay between Player X1 and their dribbler by sliding their feet, not crossing them. Encourage the dribbler to use good visual scanning to learn where the defender is located.

29. Hook-on Dribbling

Purpose: To use change of speed and direction when dribbling to move through and create open spaces while under subtle defensive pressure.

Number of Players: 12
Equipment: 4 game spots, 12 basketballs
Time: 8 to 10 minutes

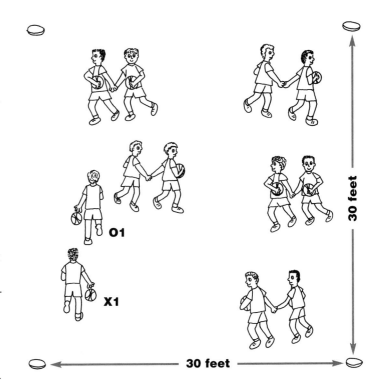

1. Players are positioned in a scattered partner formation in a 30- by 30-foot grid with inside hands held.
2. The players in one set of partners are separated. Player X1 is "it" and chases the other partner, Player O1.
3. To be saved, Player O1 must dribble the ball to another set of players and hook on to the outside arm of one player, forming a new partnership.
4. The player whose partner just got hooked onto becomes the new Player O1 and must dribble to another set of partners to be saved before Player X1 can catch him.
5. If Player O1 is caught by Player X1, then Player O1 becomes the new Player X1 and is "it."

This game requires good dribbling techniques, including changing speed and direction. Players being chased must use good visual techniques to make sound tactical decisions concerning movement into open spaces. To increase the difficulty of the game for intermediate players, have two players acting as Player X1 and two players as Player O1.

DRIBBLING DRILLS

30. Four-Team Tag Dribbling

Purpose: To develop change of direction when dribbling while under subtle defensive pressure.

Number of Players: 13
Equipment: 4 game spots, 12 basketballs
Time: 8 to 10 minutes

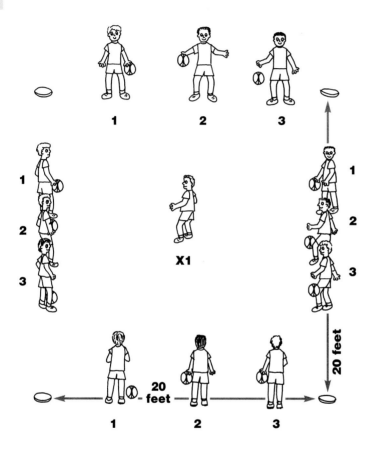

1. Position four teams of three players on a 20- by 20-foot grid so that one team is on each sideline.
2. Each team has a Player 1, Player 2, and Player 3.
3. Place the player not on a team in the middle of the grid as the defender, Player X1.
4. On your signal, Player X1 calls out a number from 1 to 3.
5. If Player X1 calls out "1," Player 1 on each team must dribble her ball across the grid and exchange places with another Player 1. Players make this exchange simultaneously.
6. Player X1 tries to tag as many players as she can before they reach the side of the grid.
7. If a player is tagged, she must sit down in the grid.
8. A tagged player may be released by a teammate who dribbles past and touches her on the head.
9. The team with the most players left after 2 minutes is the winner.
10. Scramble the teams, select a new Player X1, and repeat the action.

Coaches who have fewer than 13 players may use four teams of two as a variation. Odd numbers of players may take turns being defenders. Encourage players to dribble to open spaces away from defenders.

31. Number Tag Dribbling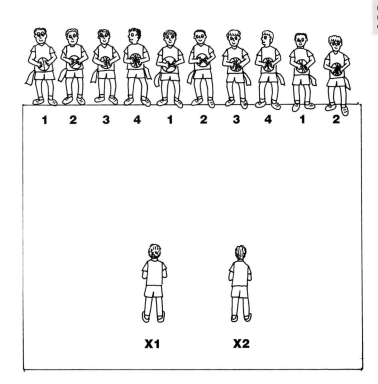

Purpose: To develop dribble penetration skills while under subtle defensive pressure.

Number of Players: 12
Equipment: 12 basketballs, 12 jerseys
Time: 8 to 10 minutes

1. Players line up on the sideline of the court and count off from one through four down the line.
2. Each player tucks a jersey in the side of his pants.
3. Two defenders, Players X1 and X2, stand between the line of players and the opposite sideline. (The space created is safe territory.)
4. The defenders call out number 1, 2, 3, or 4.
5. Those players whose number is called try to dribble to the safe line.
6. If a player has his jersey pulled while traveling to the safe line, he must go to the sideline and do 10 repetitions of a specific ball-handling skill. He may then reenter the game.

Encourage players to practice good visual scanning habits to avoid collisions with other players. It's also important to emphasize change of direction and speed as a method of creating open space and closing the opponent's space.

32. Three-Line Dribbling

Purpose: To develop dribbling penetration skills while under subtle defensive pressure.	**Number of Players:** 12 **Equipment:** 6 game spots, 9 basketballs, 3 baskets **Time:** 8 to 10 minutes

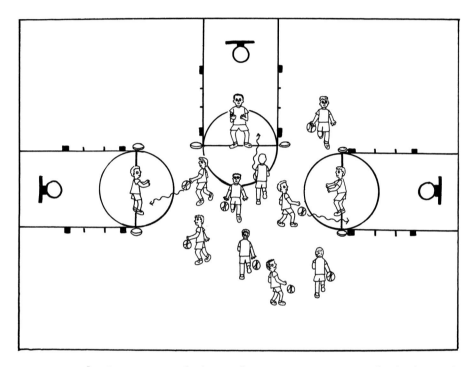

1. Position a game spot at each end of the foul line. Use three baskets for this drill.

2. Position one player on each foul line between the game spots.

3. The other players hold basketballs and are scattered randomly on the court.

4. On your signal, three of the scattered players dribble toward the basket of their choice, one player at each basket.

5. Each dribbler attempts to dribble between the game spots and get past the defender, who must stay on the foul line. Once past the defender, the dribbler continues to the basket and then dribbles to another basket.

6. Next, the remaining three dribblers repeat the action of trying to dribble past the defenders.

7. After 2 minutes select three new defenders and repeat the sequence.

When ready, players must be challenged with some defensive pressure. By allowing the defenders to move only laterally along the foul line, the pressure is somewhat subtle. Encourage players to use good feinting and change of lateral direction to beat the defender.

33. Two-Team Tag Dribbling

Purpose: To develop change of direction when dribbling while under subtle defensive pressure.	**Number of Players:** 12 **Equipment:** 4 game spots, 12 basketballs, 6 red jerseys, 6 blue jerseys **Time:** 8 to 10 minutes

1. Divide the players into two teams. Position the players in a 30- by 30-foot grid and have players tuck a jersey in the back of their shorts.
2. One player from each team will be designated as the tagger and will wear her jersey.
3. On your signal, all players begin dribbling throughout the grid.
4. If a tagger tags a player from the opposite team, that player must sit down and continue dribbling.
5. While sitting, this tagged player may not move from that space but may tag members of the opposite team.
6. The last team to have a dribbler left who is not a tagger is the winner.
7. Change taggers and repeat the action.

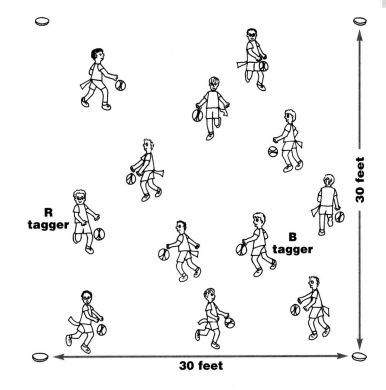

Two-Team Tag Dribbling provides opportunities for players to develop skill at changing direction and speed while dribbling. Encourage players to use good visual habits to find open spaces and avoid collisions. For variation in the game, the tagger might play without a ball, the tagger might dribble two balls, or everyone but the tagger might dribble two balls.

34. Freeze Tag Dribbling

Purpose: To move into open space while under subtle and increasing defensive pressure.

Number of Players: 12
Equipment: 4 game spots, 8 basketballs, 4 red jerseys
Time: 5 to 7 minutes

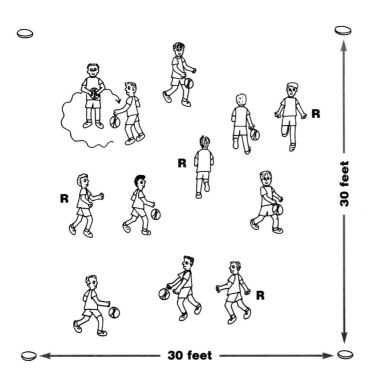

30 feet

30 feet

1. Position players in a scattered formation throughout a 30- by 30-foot grid. Four of the players wear a red jersey and don't have a ball. They are taggers (defenders).

2. On your signal, each tagger tries to touch a player who is dribbling a ball. If successful, that player must freeze, and the tagger goes after someone else. The taggers try to freeze the entire group.

3. If a player dribbling a ball is frozen, he may be rescued by one of the other players, who dribbles around the frozen player in a circle.

4. After everyone is frozen, or after 3 minutes have elapsed, change taggers and repeat the sequence.

This simple game provides lots of opportunities for decision making. Encourage players to use good visual scanning techniques to avoid closed spaces and red-shirted taggers. Between games offer players a short time to rest as you ask them how changing directions, speeds, and levels can help them to be successful when dribbling. If the players have beginning dribbling skills, you might limit the movement of the taggers to skipping, galloping, or jumping.

DRIBBLING DRILLS

35. One-on-One Dribbling

Purpose: To use change of speed and direction when dribbling to reach a specific destination while under gamelike pressure.

Number of Players: 2
Equipment: 4 game spots, 1 basketball
Time: 5 to 7 minutes

1. Position four game spots to form a 15- by 15-foot grid.
2. Player O1 has the ball and stands by game spot A.
3. Player X1 is the defender and stands by game spot C, which is diagonal to game spot A.
4. Player X1 asks Player O1 if she is ready and, if yes, tries to touch Player O1's ball.
5. Player O1 tries to dribble over game spot B or game spot D.
6. Player X1 earns 1 point if Player O1 turns her back or if Player X1 touches the ball or creates a turnover (due to such factors as a double dribble, loss of control, or dribbling out of the grid). Player O1 earns 1 point if she is able to dribble over either game spot. The winner is the player who gets to 3 points first. Players then exchange roles and play again.

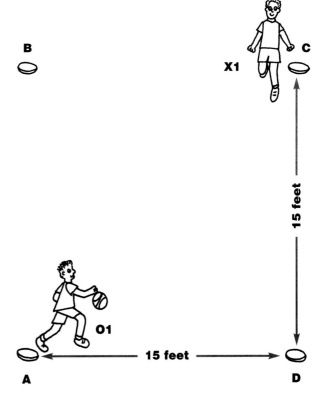

This drill promotes the offensive skill of dribbling toward one spot and quickly changing direction by teaching players to use the head, hips, and shoulders for feinting. Players should also be encouraged to move to both the left and right and not just toward their dominant side. To reward players for using their nondominant side, double the amount of points earned when players use their nondominant hand to dribble. Many beginning players want to turn their backs to the defender rather than using a change of direction to create an open space. This drill forces players to take on a defender without turning their back. Explain that the dribbler who turns her back loses visual clues to help in decision making. Advanced players will be more challenged in this drill if the size of the grid is reduced.

DRIBBLING DRILLS

36. Baseball Dribbling

Purpose: To develop dribbling skills while under gamelike defensive pressure.

Number of Players: 2
Equipment: 8 game spots, 1 basketball
Time: 8 to 10 minutes

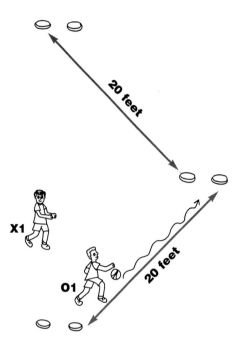

1. Position the game spots approximately 20 feet apart in the shape of a baseball diamond.
2. The defender, Player X1, passes the ball to Player O1 to begin the action.
3. Player O1 tries to dribble the ball between the game spots at first, second, or third base. She earns 1 point by dribbling through the game spots at first base, 2 points at second base, and 3 points at third base.
4. Player O1 earns 4 points by dribbling through any of the bases and returning home safely.
5. If Player X1 touches the ball or creates a turnover, she earns an out.
6. After three outs, players reverse roles and play again.

Encourage players with the ball to change direction and speed so they can create space and score points. If scoring is too hard for players, widen the space between the game spots used as bases. If defenders are having trouble getting outs, reduce the size of the playing area or set a point limit.

37. Jersey Tag Dribbling

Purpose: To use change of speed and direction to move through and create open space when dribbling while under gamelike defensive pressure.

Number of Players: 5 to 7
Equipment: 4 game spots, 5 to 7 basketballs, 5 to 7 jerseys
Time: 5 to 7 minutes

1. Scatter players, each with a basketball, in a 20- by 20-foot grid.
2. All players have jerseys tucked in the back of their shorts.
3. Players try to "get away" from all of the other players by moving through the grid and changing speed and direction as they dribble.
4. As they practice evasive measures, players also try to grab a jersey from another player.
5. If a player's jersey is grabbed, the jersey is returned, and that player must go out of the grid and perform a ball-handling skill before returning to the game.
6. Winners may be determined by the number of jerseys grabbed or the number of times a player has gone out.

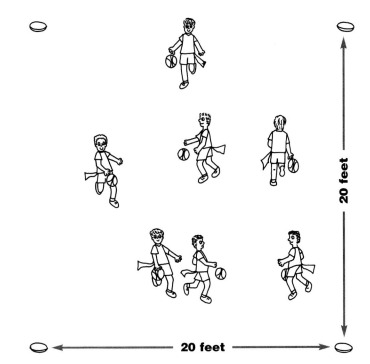

If players commit a violation (such as a double dribble or carrying the ball), or if they lose control of the ball when trying to grab a jersey, they are out. Vary the skill that players must perform in order to return to the game, such as leg circles, dribbling with the nondominant hand, or crossovers. This drill is considered gamelike defensively because all participants are defenders.

38. Double Trouble Dribbling

Purpose: To move into open space when dribbling while under increasing defensive pressure.	**Number of Players:** 12 **Equipment:** 4 game spots, 10 basketballs **Time:** 5 to 7 minutes

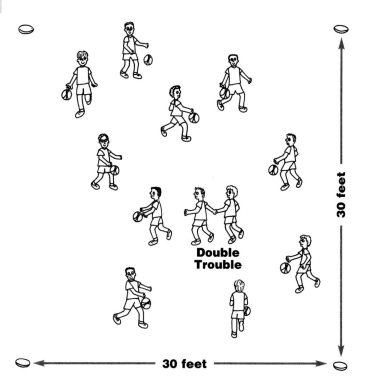

30 feet

30 feet

Double Trouble

1. Position players in a scattered formation throughout a 30- by 30-foot grid.
2. Select two players to be Double Trouble—they will be taggers but won't have a ball.
3. Double Trouble hold hands and chase the other players, who must dribble their ball and run away so they aren't tagged.
4. When the first player is tagged by Double Trouble, he must put his ball outside the playing area and hold hands with one of the Double Trouble pair. The Double Trouble threesome now continue trying to catch the other players.
5. When a second player is caught (bringing Double Trouble up to four players), the taggers split and make two groups of Double Trouble.
6. The game continues with Double Trouble splitting into another group each time the group reaches four players.
7. The last dribbler left is the winner.

Dribblers need good visual scanning techniques to continue to move into open spaces and avoid all of the Double Troubles. This simple game can be used to begin teaching players how to avoid being trapped by pressure defenses.

39. Multiplication Tag Dribbling 👉

Purpose: To use change of direction and speed to move through and create open spaces while under increasing gamelike defensive pressure.

Number of Players: 12
Equipment: 4 game spots, 11 basketballs
Time: 5 to 7 minutes

1. Select one player to be "it." This player doesn't have a ball.
2. Scatter all the other players, each with a basketball, in a 30- by 30-foot grid.
3. On your signal, "it" tries to tag a player. When a player is tagged, she must put her ball outside the grid and help "it" tag other players.
4. When only one player is left who has not been tagged, this player is the winner.

This game is extremely challenging, even for the more experienced players. As the number of defenders increases, tactical decisions concerning use of space become more complicated. The game presents opportunities for players to continue developing vision and movement skills.

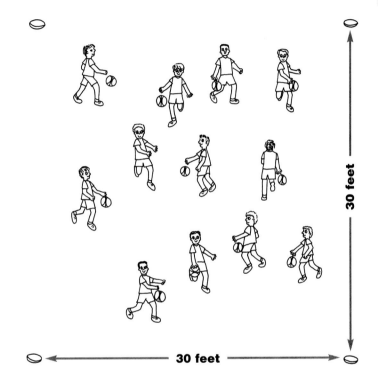

30 feet

30 feet

DRIBBLING DRILLS

40. Six-Chute Dribbling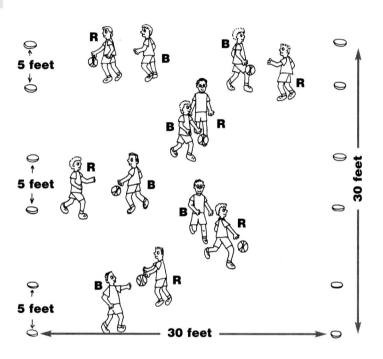

Purpose: To create an open space to dribble through while under game-like defensive pressure.

Number of Players: 12
Equipment: 12 game spots, 6 basketballs, 6 red jerseys, 6 blue jerseys
Time: 8 to 10 minutes

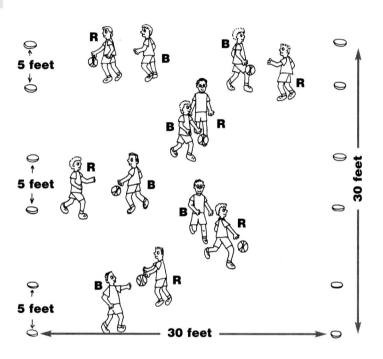

1. In a 30- by 30-foot grid, position 12 game spots so that they make three sets of 5-foot-wide chutes on each end of the court.
2. Divide players into two teams, red and blue, and have them put on the appropriately colored jersey.
3. Each player from the red team pairs up with a player from the blue team. Each pair has a basketball.
4. On your signal, the player in each pair with the ball tries to dribble the ball through one of the chutes on the opposite side of the court. He may select any one of the three chutes to dribble through.
5. If he makes it through the chute, he receives 1 point for his team. Then he tries to dribble to the opposite side of the court and score again by dribbling through a chute on that side.
6. Play continues until the defender can steal the ball or there is a dribbling violation. In either case, the players switch roles, and the other player tries to dribble through a chute.
7. The game continues for 2 minutes, at which time the team with the highest number of points is the winner.

All 12 players are playing at the same time, so players must practice good visual scanning to reduce the possibility of collision. To begin the game, make sure half of the balls go to each team. If there is an odd number of pairs, let the players shoot foul shots to determine which team gets the additional ball. This game is more fast paced when players are not allowed to turn their backs to the defender when dribbling.

41. One-on-One-on-One Dribbling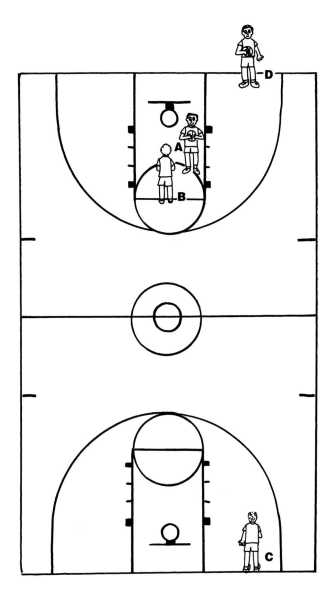

Purpose: To develop dribble penetration skills while under gamelike defensive pressure.

Number of Players: 4
Equipment: 3 basketballs, 2 baskets
Time: 8 to 10 minutes

1. Position Player A under the basket with a ball and ready to dribble to the opposite end of the court and shoot.
2. Position Player B at the foul line.
3. On your signal, Player A dribbles to the opposite end of the court and shoots while Player B defends.
4. If Player A makes the basket, she becomes the new defender. Player B goes off the court, and Player C, who was waiting under the basket, dribbles to the opposite end and shoots while being defended by Player A.
5. Player D, who was waiting under the opposite basket, becomes the new offensive player while Player C now defends.
6. If the offensive player misses the shot and fails to get the rebound, she automatically becomes the defender.
7. If the defender steals the ball at any time, she becomes the offensive player.

This drill is great for developing full-court dribbling skills with speed and defensive pressure. Because of the high intensity, side baskets should be used to help diminish the fatigue factor. Variations of this drill have the players required to finish with a particular type of shot, such as a layup or jump shot.

42. Zigzag Dribbling

Purpose: To develop dribble penetration skills while under gamelike defensive pressure.

Number of Players: 8
Equipment: 4 basketballs, 2 baskets
Time: 5 to 7 minutes

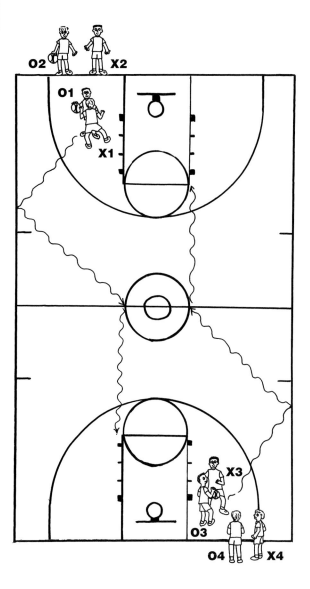

1. Position two offensive players and two defensive players under each basket.
2. On your signal, Player O1 dribbles diagonally toward the sideline, then back to the middle of the court, and then back to the junction of the midcourt line and sideline in a zigzag fashion. Player X1 aggressively defends.
3. At the same time, Player O3 begins an identical movement from the opposite side of the court while being defended by Player X3.
4. As the offensive players reach the half-court line, the next set of partners begins to dribble in a similar manner.
5. When the offensive players reach the half-court line, they explode to the basket, dribbling in any pathway they choose in an effort to score.
6. Players then reverse roles and repeat the actions.

Emphasize that offensive players should keep their bodies between the ball and the defenders when executing the zigzag pattern. They should maintain a good dribbling stance with legs flexed and head up for good vision. After reaching half-court, each dribbler should try to break contact with the defender by changing speed and direction quickly. Once a dribbler has created space between herself and the defender, she may use a variety of dribbling techniques such as the crossover or reverse dribble to keep the defender off balance. For safety purposes, have dribblers explode to the basket using one side of the court only so that they don't collide with another set of players.

43. One-on-Two Possession

Purpose: To keep possession of the ball while under intense defensive pressure.	**Number of Players:** 3 **Equipment:** 4 game spots, 1 basketball **Time:** 3 to 5 minutes

1. Position three players in a 15-by 15-foot grid so that Player O1 has the ball and Players X1 and X2 are defenders.
2. On your signal, Player O1 tries to maintain possession for 15 seconds by changing direction and speed.
3. At the end of 15 seconds, players change roles and repeat the action.

This drill helps players improve their quickness in changing directions and speed. Good visual habits should be encouraged to determine the position of defenders and the availability of open space. Use several grids to accommodate the number of players available.

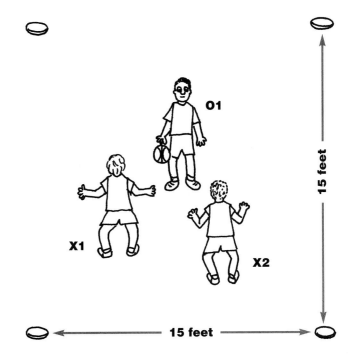

DRIBBLING DRILLS

44. One-on-Two Direction Dribbling

Purpose: To develop dribble penetration skills while under intense defensive pressure.

Number of Players: 3
Equipment: 4 game spots, 1 basketball
Time: 5 to 7 minutes

1. Position three players in a 15-by 15-foot grid so that Player O1 has the ball and Players X1 and X2 are defenders.
2. Player O1 stands on a line between two game spots on one side of the grid while Players X1 and X2 are on the opposite side.
3. On your signal, Player O1 tries to dribble across the line where the defenders are standing. If he does, he receives 2 points.
4. If one of the defenders stops Player O1 by touching the ball or creating a turnover, that defender receives 1 point.
5. Whoever scores 4 points first is the winner.
6. Change roles and repeat the action.

This is an offensive drill, so more points are awarded for the offensive effort of crossing the defenders' line. When working with players during this or any other offensive drill, limit comments to issues concerning dribbling, change of direction, speed, and so on. Use more than one grid if more players are available.

45. One-on-Two Half-Court Dribbling

Purpose: To develop dribble penetration skills while under intense defensive pressure.	**Number of Players:** 6 **Equipment:** 2 basketballs, 1 basket **Time:** 8 to 10 minutes

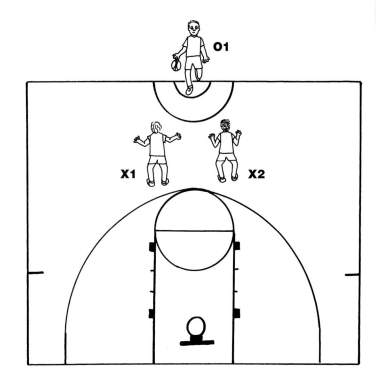

1. Position two sets of three players at the half-court line so that each set has one offensive player, O1, and two defensive players, X1 and X2.
2. Only one set of players is active at a time.
3. On your signal, Player O1 has 10 seconds to try to beat Players X1 and X2 to the basket and score.
4. The second set of players then repeats the action, with its Player O1 trying to score and Players X1 and X2 trying to prevent the basket. The first set of players returns to the half-court line, and a new player becomes Player O1.
5. Repeat the action several times, giving the offensive player 3 points each time she is able to score and 2 points each time she is able to take a shot.
6. Award defenders 1 point each time they successfully stop Player O1 from shooting.
7. The player with the most points wins the game.

This drill challenges even the most accomplished dribblers. Encourage players to keep their heads up for good vision as they dribble. If more players are available, use both ends of the court at the same time. You may want to restrict this drill to the guards on one half of the court while the forwards are completing "big men" drills (drills for forwards and centers) on the other end.

CHAPTER 5

Passing Drills

Teams that demonstrate good passing skills help to reduce or eliminate turnovers, which translates into more shot opportunities each game. Players need hundreds of opportunities each practice in small-group situations to develop solid passing techniques of the chest pass, bounce pass, baseball pass, and overhead pass.

When teaching the *chest pass*, encourage players to place their hands on the sides of the ball, thumbs pointing toward each other and slightly upward. As players pass the ball from chest level to their partners, they step forward to generate more force. As they step, they snap their wrists with thumbs pointing downward.

The *bounce pass* is executed in basically the same manner except that the ball is bounced between the passer and receiver so that it can be received at about waist height. I like to tell my beginning players to pass from the belly button so they avoid raising their arms and bouncing the ball too high. The pass may be executed using one or two hands. It is probably the best pass for beginning players because it reduces the fear factor. Players are not afraid of being struck in the face with the ball because it is bounced at waist level. The bounce pass also forces teammates to move to support positions because players can't throw over defenders when using the bounce pass.

The *baseball pass*, used primarily by intermediate and advanced players, provides an excellent way to pass quickly and accurately for both short- and long-distance passing. Emphasize that players should bring the throwing hand behind the ear (especially younger players who will have to use two hands), rotate the hips and shoulders as much as possible without moving the pivot foot, and rapidly extend the throwing hand in a forward motion.

The two-hand *overhead pass* is the most difficult because it requires the most wrist strength. It is used mostly by older, more physically developed players. Emphasize keeping the ball high over the head with two hands, stepping forward, and snapping the wrists as the arms accelerate from a backward to forward motion.

Players need to develop these passing skills in a developmentally appropriate progression, from a stationary player passing to a stationary player, to a stationary player passing to a moving player, and then a moving player passing to a moving player. Players should have time to practice these skills while under no defensive pressure, increasing to subtle defensive pressure, and finally gamelike pressure.

Incorporated in the design of the drills are opportunities to combine skill acquisition with decision making. Decision-making opportunities are essential because it is not good enough for players to know the proper chest-pass technique if they don't know when to use it. To assist in this decision-making process, many of the passing drills in this chapter use grids to structure space for learning. The drills performed in the grids are designed to help players improve communication, vision, and timing of their movements. Improvement in these areas in small-group work will lead to improvement in the players' ability to connect passes.

Players should have many early opportunities to practice passing techniques with the nondominant hand. As they progress, you can make the drills more difficult by gradually changing the time, space, and defensive pressure and calling for higher level tactical decision making.

46. Triangle Passing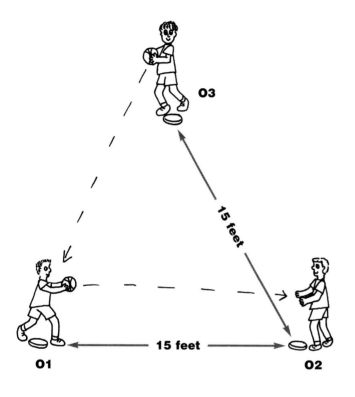

Purpose: To develop eye-hand coordination and visual tracking for passing skills while under no defensive pressure.

Number of Players: 3
Equipment: 3 game spots, 2 basketballs
Time: 3 to 5 minutes

O3

15 feet

15 feet

O1

O2

1. Position three game spots in a triangle formation 15 feet apart.
2. Position one player at each game spot. Two of the players have a ball.
3. On your signal, Player O1 passes the ball to Player O2.
4. As soon as Player O1 releases the ball, Player O3 passes the ball to Player O1, so that the balls are always in motion.
5. Repeat the action for 1 minute.

After 1 minute of action, change the type of pass required. Players might start with a bounce pass and then move on to chest pass, one-hand pass right side, one-hand pass left side, two-hand pass above head. Insist that the player passing the ball wait for visual contact from the receiver before passing. To enhance communication skills, players might call out the name of the player they're passing to.

47. Partner Passing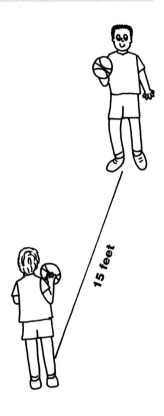

Purpose: To develop eye-hand coordination and visual tracking for passing skills while under no defensive pressure.

Number of Players: 2
Equipment: 2 basketballs
Time: 3 to 5 minutes

1. Position two players 15 feet apart.
2. On your signal, players continually pass the ball with their right hand to their partner.
3. Continue the action for 30 seconds.
4. Players repeat the action using the left hand for passing.
5. Have players keep track of how many consecutive passes they can make without a fumble.

Players should pass at a rate of speed that is commensurate with their skill level. Passing with accuracy is more important than speed. Variations for this drill include passing with a bounce pass and one-partner chest pass while the other partner uses a bounce pass. As passing efficiency increases, players should count the number of passes they can make in 30 seconds. You may want to record results weekly to evaluate player progress.

15 feet

PASSING DRILLS

48. Pass and Move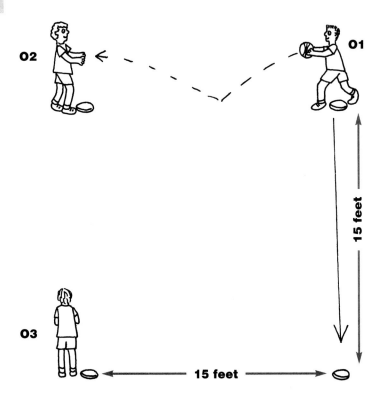

Purpose: To help initiate the concept of pass and move while under no defensive pressure.	**Number of Players:** 3 **Equipment:** 4 game spots, 1 basketball **Time:** 5 to 7 minutes

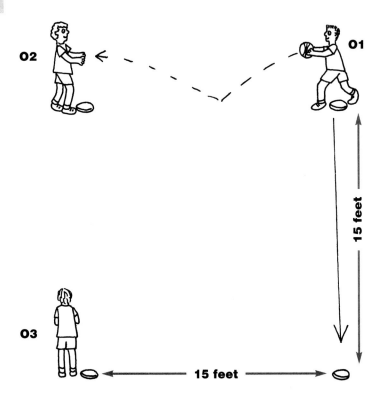

1. Position four game spots to form a 15- by 15-foot grid.
2. Three players each occupy a corner of the grid.
3. On your signal, Player O1 passes to Player O2 and then moves to the unoccupied corner.
4. Next Player O2 passes to Player O3 and then moves to the corner previously occupied by Player O1.
5. Continue this action.

Beginning players must understand that after they pass the ball, they must move and be ready to receive the ball back. Insist that players make good eye contact when passing and communicate by calling the name of the player they're passing to.

49. Move to Support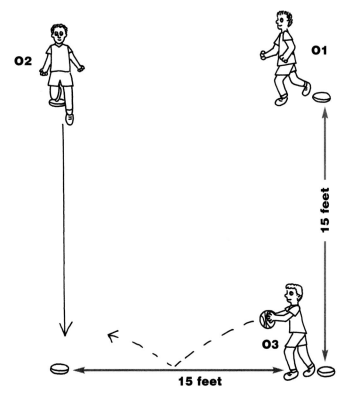

Purpose: To initiate the concept of movement to a support position while under no defensive pressure.

Number of Players: 3
Equipment: 4 game spots, 1 basketball
Time: 5 to 7 minutes

1. Position four game spots to form a 15- by 15-foot grid.
2. Each player occupies a game spot.
3. On your signal, Player O2, the player without the ball closest to the empty corner, moves to the open space (open corner) and shouts out "Space."
4. Player O3 passes the ball to Player O2.
5. Player O1 then moves to the open corner and receives a pass from Player O2.
6. Repeat the action.

Encourage players to make eye contact with the player who has the ball before they move to space. Shouting "Space" helps initiate the communication skills necessary for successful play. Insist that players who are being passed to collect the ball, immediately assume a triple-threat position, look by using visual scanning, and decide to dribble, pass, or shoot, according to situation presented. This process of collect—look—make a decision is the foundation for the beginning of intentional play.

PASSING DRILLS

50. Group Pass and Move

Purpose: To initiate the concept of pass and move, when faced with visual distractions and while under no defensive pressure.

Number of Players: 12
Equipment: 4 game spots, 4 basketballs
Time: 5 to 7 minutes

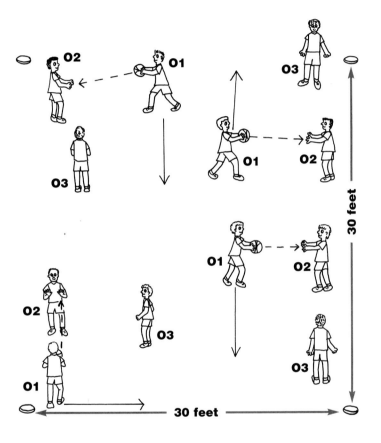

1. Position four game spots to form a 30- by 30-foot grid.
2. Position four groups of three players in the grid with a ball.
3. In each group, Player O1 passes to Player O2 and then moves to an open space anywhere in the grid.
4. Player O2 passes to Player O3 and moves to an open space.
5. Player O1 calls for the ball from Player O3, who passes it back to Player O1.
6. Players continue the action for 1 minute and then change the style of pass.
7. Have players count the number of consecutive passes they can make without a turnover.

This drill challenges the visual scanning skills of the players as they pass and relocate to an open space, because there are four players moving at the same time. Communication and passing accuracy are necessary for consecutive passes. Players receiving passes should move away from the ball (feinting) initially and then change direction quickly as they come back to the ball.

51. Diagonal Passing

Purpose: To develop passing accuracy from a stationary player to a moving player while under no defensive pressure.

Number of Players: 4
Equipment: 2 game spots, 1 basketball
Time: 5 to 7 minutes

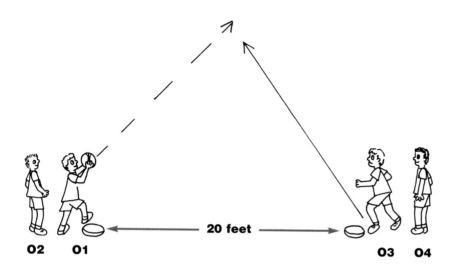

1. Position two game spots 20 feet apart.
2. Two players stand behind each spot.
3. On your signal, Player O3 makes a diagonal run either left or right.
4. Player O1 passes to the space that O3 is moving toward.
5. Player O3 collects the ball, pivots, and passes it back to Player O4. Player O3 then sprints behind Player O4.
6. Player O4 then passes to a moving Player O1, who collects the ball, pivots, and passes it back to Player O2. Then Player O1 sprints behind Player O2.
7. Repeat the action.

Before attempting this drill, you'll need to demonstrate a pass in which the passer has to lead the receiver. This type of pass is more difficult for beginning players than a pass from a stationary passer to a stationary target. Key aspects of the lead pass include the distance between passer and receiver, the speed of the receiver, and the speed of the pass. To encourage communication skills, have receivers call for the ball as they move to open space. Emphasize the use of the forward pivot, reverse pivot, and jump stop (either foot may be the pivot foot) during this drill.

52. Circle Passing

Purpose: To develop passing accuracy from a stationary player to a moving player while under no defensive pressure.

Number of Players: 12
Equipment: 4 game spots, 6 basketballs
Time: 5 to 7 minutes

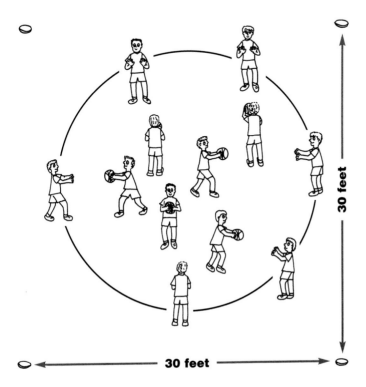

30 feet

← 30 feet →

1. Position four game spots in a 30- by 30-foot grid.
2. Divide players into two groups, with one group forming a circle and the other group scattered inside the circle with the balls.
3. On your signal, each player inside the circle dribbles the ball through open space, finds a player on the circle to receive a pass, makes visual contact with this player and calls out his name, and then passes.
4. After passing, each player inside the circle moves away to another space in the grid, makes visual contact with another player on the circle, and receives a pass.
5. Players repeat this action for 1 minute and then switch roles.

Players are challenged to complete accurate passes because of the other players moving in the grid. Visual scanning and communication will reduce the possibility of collision and enhance passing accuracy. To make a game out of this drill, see which player can pass to all six players on the circle and sit down first.

53. Return to Passer

Purpose: To develop passing accuracy from a stationary player to a moving player while under no defensive pressure.

Number of Players: 12
Equipment: 4 game spots, 6 basketballs, 6 blue jerseys, 6 red jerseys
Time: 8 to 10 minutes

1. Position four game spots to form a 30- by 30-foot grid.
2. Scatter six red players in the grid, who will remain stationary.
3. Position six blue players in the grid with basketballs.
4. On your signal, the blue players dribble through the grid. When a blue player approaches a stationary red player, she makes eye contact and passes the ball.
5. After passing, this blue player waits until the red player collects the ball. Then she changes direction quickly and calls for the ball. The red player passes the ball back to the blue player, who repeats the action with another player.
6. Continue the action for 1 minute and then reverse roles.

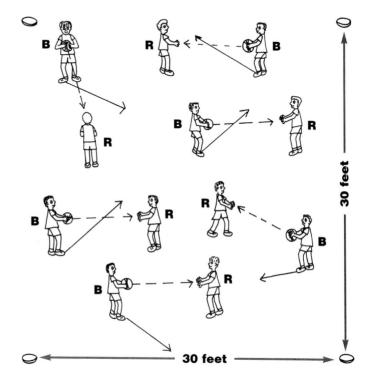

The number of players moving at the same time adds a visual complication to the drill. Encourage players to use good visual scanning techniques. Player movements should be crisp, and players should be encouraged to move at different angles to receive passes. This is an excellent drill for practicing the jump stop and pivot before passing to a stationary player.

54. Number Passing

Purpose: To develop passing accuracy from a moving player to a moving player while under no defensive pressure.

Number of Players: 12
Equipment: 4 game spots, 2 basketballs, 6 red jerseys, 6 blue jerseys
Time: 8 to 10 minutes

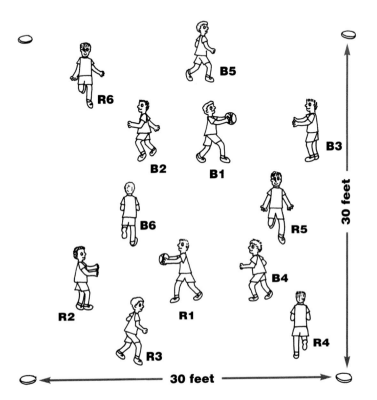

1. Position four game spots to form a 30- by 30-foot grid.
2. Divide players into six red players and six blue players.
3. Number each group of players from one to six.
4. Give Player 1 on each team a ball.
5. On your signal, all players move freely throughout the grid. Player 1 must pass to Player 2 on the same team and move to open space.
6. Player 2 from each team passes to Player 3, Player 3 to Player 4, Player 4 to Player 5, Player 5 to Player 6, and Player 6 to Player 1.
7. Players repeat the action.

Emphasize the use of the entire grid for passing. Visual scanning will help prevent passing into a closed space (another player). Encourage the use of several types of passes. As players become more efficient with this drill, start a ball with Players 1 and 3 in each group. The second ball within each group tends to slow the pace of play. Insist that players move vigorously and communicate with each other for better results.

55. Star Passing

Purpose: To develop passing accuracy and decision making while under subtle defensive pressure.

Number of Players: 6
Equipment: 4 game spots, 1 basketball
Time: 5 to 7 minutes

1. Position four game spots to form a 20- by 20-foot grid.
2. Position five players in a star formation within the grid.
3. Player X1 assumes a defensive position inside of the star.
4. On your signal, the players pass the ball to another player in the star while the defender tries to touch the ball.
5. Players must pass the ball to either of the players across from them, rather than to either of the players beside them.
6. If Player X1 touches the ball, he earns his way out of the star, and the player who allowed the touch must take his place.
7. Players keep track of how many consecutive passes they can make without the defender touching the ball.

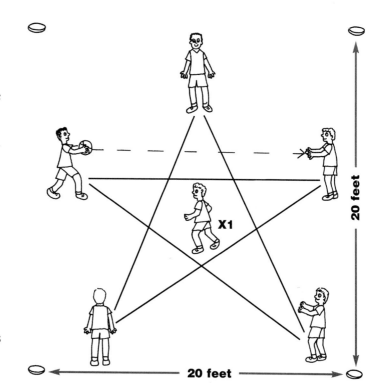

Players should use pass fakes to create spaces to pass. A variety of passes—including chest, bounce, baseball, and two-hand overhead—should be alternated during the drill. Although having just one defender is not very gamelike, players will need to use decision-making skills to determine where to pass the ball.

56. Three-on-None, Two-on-One Passing

Purpose: To develop passing accuracy from a moving player to a moving player while under subtle defensive pressure.

Number of Players: 6
Equipment: 2 baskets, 2 basketballs
Time: 8 to 10 minutes

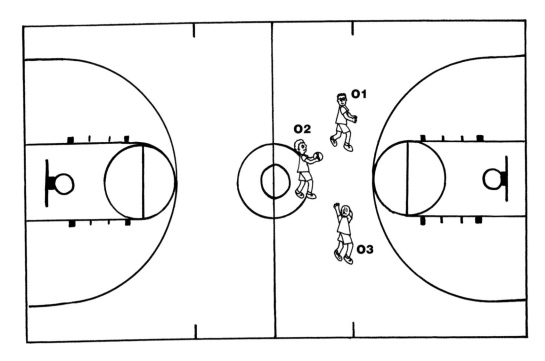

1. Position two lines of three players behind basket A.
2. The three players from line 1 pass the ball to each other as they move toward basket B (the illustration shows Player O2 passing to O3).
3. One of the players, in this example O3, shoots a layup to finish.
4. As soon as the shot is taken, Player O3 sprints back to basket A and becomes the defender, X1.
5. Players O1 and O2 now have a two-on-one fast-break opportunity in the other direction.
6. After the shot is taken, the next line of players repeats the action.

Change the passing pattern when the three players are moving toward basket B to include players moving in straight lines, weaving, or moving freely. Encourage players to move at full speed and and to pass to spaces accurately. Since this is a passing drill, limit your coaching comments to passing skills only.

57. Three-on-One Keep Away

Purpose: To help develop the concept of moving without the ball to a support position while under subtle defensive pressure.	**Number of Players:** 4 **Equipment:** 4 game spots, 1 basketball **Time:** 8 to 10 minutes

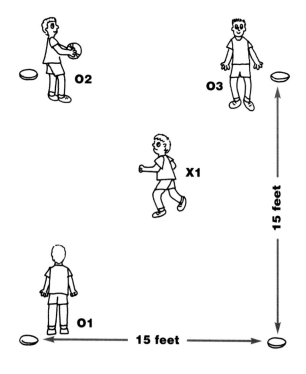

1. Place four game spots in a 15- by 15-foot grid.
2. Position players so that they occupy three corners of the grid and one player is in the middle as a defender.
3. The defender's role is to touch the ball or cause another player to make a mistake, such as a pass outside the grid. If a player does make a mistake, she replaces the defender in the middle.
4. Players O1, O2, and O3 are playing a three-on-one keep-away game. They are allowed to move only to the corner space that is not occupied.
5. The perimeter players are not allowed to pass the ball across the middle of the grid.
6. Perimeter players without the ball must move to support positions for the player with the ball.
7. Players count the number of consecutive passes the perimeter players can make.
8. After 1 minute, if the defender has not touched the ball, change positions and repeat the action.

The player with the ball has a responsibility to make a good choice of where to pass. It is impossible for the defender to defend both passing lanes, so the player with the ball must decide which one is open. This activity helps players develop the process of collect, look, and make a decision. It also reinforces the concept of movement without the ball.

Insist that players use only bounce passes. This will prevent passing over the top of the defender and ensure that movement becomes the solution to the problem that the defender has presented. A variation of this activity might include the removal of the game spots as boundaries. Players could play three-on-one going to the basket and finish with a layup.

58. Double Movement Three-on-One

Purpose: To develop the concept of pass and move while under subtle defensive pressure.

Number of Players: 4
Equipment: 4 game spots, 1 basketball
Time: 8 to 10 minutes

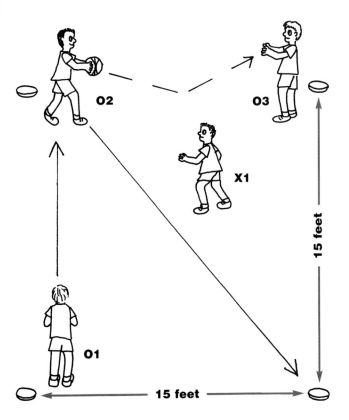

1. Position four game spots to form a 15- by 15-foot grid.
2. Position three offensive players so they occupy three corners of the grid.
3. Place one defender in the middle. His role is to apply defensive pressure to create a turnover.
4. On your signal, Player O2 uses a bounce pass to pass the ball to Player O3. Player O2 then sprints to the unoccupied corner, Player O1 moves to the space previously occupied by Player O2, and Player O3 passes to Player O1.
5. This action is repeated until the defender forces a turnover or 1 minute elapses. Change to a new defender and start again.
6. Offensive players count the number of consecutive passes without a turnover.

This drill provides the opportunity for continuous motion. The concept of moving without the ball in relationship to other offensive players will be an integral step in understanding a half-court offense.

59. Inside/Outside Three-on-One 👈

Purpose: To develop the concept of moving without the ball to a support position while under subtle defensive pressure.

Number of Players: 4
Equipment: 4 game spots, 1 basketball, 1 red jersey
Time: 8 to 10 minutes

1. Position game spots to make a 15- by 15-foot grid.
2. One offensive player, O1, stands outside the grid, and three players are inside the grid. One of the inside players is a defender, X1, and wears a jersey; the other two are offensive players, O2 and O3.
3. Player O1 passes the ball to either Player O2 or O3 inside the grid.
4. The other offensive player inside the grid must then move to open space and receive the ball. She then passes the ball back outside the grid to Player O1.
5. If Player X1 can touch the ball at any time or force a turnover, then the player who made the mistake switches roles with the defender.
6. Players have 1 minute to see how many consecutive passes can be made without error.

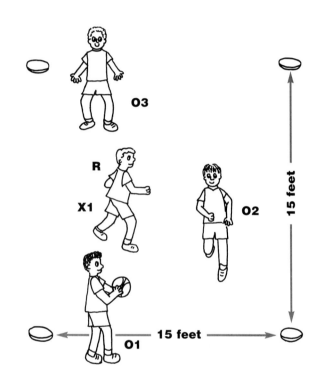

Encourage quick changes of direction and speed to create open spaces for collecting the ball. Communication and vision among players inside the grid play an important role in their success with this drill. Promote the development of solutions by asking what role communication between players has on successfully connecting passes.

PASSING DRILLS

60. Team Keep Away

Purpose: To develop the concept of moving without the ball to a support position while under subtle defensive pressure.

Number of Players: 12
Equipment: 4 game spots, 1 basketball, 4 red jerseys, 4 blue jerseys, 4 yellow jerseys
Time: 8 to 10 minutes

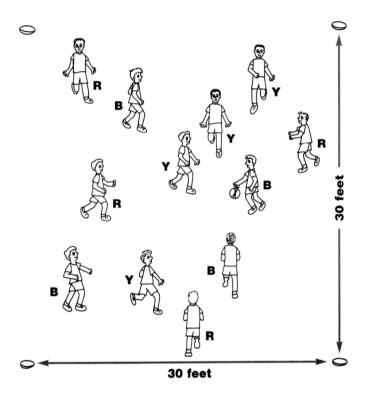

1. Position four game spots to create a 30- by 30-foot grid.
2. Players are divided into three teams of four players, are given colored jerseys to wear, and are scattered within the grid.
3. Designate two offensive teams and one defensive team.
4. The two offensive teams try to keep the ball away from the defensive team.
5. If the defensive team touches the ball or causes a turnover, the team responsible for the mistake becomes the new defensive team.

Players should be encouraged to move to open space to provide support when their team is in possession of the ball. Players should constantly scan to help with spacing of players. Get your players thinking by asking them what happens when more than one player from the same team occupies the same space.

61. Partner Direction

> **Purpose:** To develop the concept of movement without the ball to a support position while under subtle defensive pressure.
>
> **Number of Players:** 3
> **Equipment:** 4 game spots, 1 basketball, 1 red jersey
> **Time:** 8 to 10 minutes

1. Position the game spots to create a 20- by 20-foot grid.
2. Position two offensive players at one end of the grid.
3. One defensive player wears a red jersey and positions himself anywhere in the grid he feels is appropriate.
4. The offensive players pass the ball to each other while attempting to cross an imaginary line between the markers at the opposite end of the grid. (Players pass the ball, then move to a new space closer to the imaginary line. They may not take steps when in possession of the ball.) Each time they are successful, they receive 1 point.
5. If the defender touches the ball or there is a violation, such as a 5-second held-ball violation or the ball is passed out of the grid, the defender switches roles with the offensive player responsible for the error.
6. No dribbling is allowed.

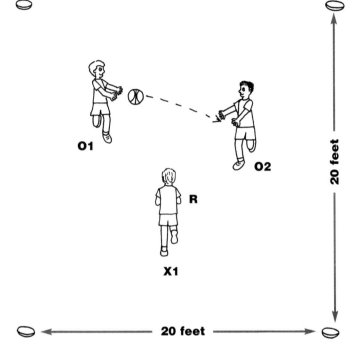

Encourage the offensive players to change speed and direction to create spaces that will allow them to penetrate the territory being defended in order to reach the opposite end of the grid. After players begin to develop the concept of movement without the ball, increase the level of difficulty by adding more players to make a three-on-two situation. Then increase the size of the grid appropriate to the players' skill level. A guiding notion to promote thinking is how movement creates opportunities for success.

62. Two-Circle Passing

Purpose: To develop an understanding of passing accuracy and decision making while under subtle defensive pressure.

Number of Players: 12
Equipment: 8 game spots, 2 basketballs, 6 red jerseys, 6 blue jerseys
Time: 6 to 8 minutes

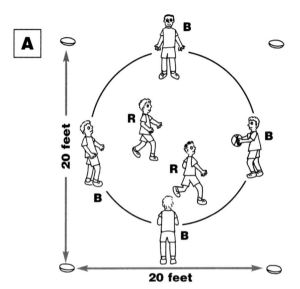

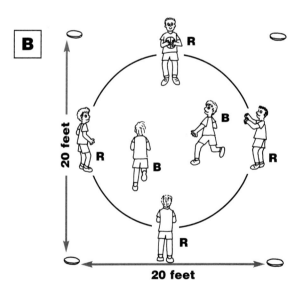

1. Position eight game spots to make two 20- by 20-foot grids.
2. Position four players in a circle formation inside each grid. One circle has blue players and the other red players.
3. Place two red defenders in the blue circle and two blue defenders in the red circle.
4. On your signal, the players in the circle begin passing the ball while the defenders try to touch it or intercept a pass.
5. If the defender from the circle in grid A touches a ball, then the player who made the mistake, a blue player, must go to the circle in grid B and take the place of one of the blue defenders. The blue defender who was replaced then rejoins her own circle of blue players in grid A.
6. As this action is repeated, players from each circle count how many consecutive passes they can make without a mistake. They must begin a new count each time a defender touches the ball or there is a bad pass. The team with the most consecutive passes is the winner.

Emphasize the need for passing accuracy as players collect the ball, look around them, and make quick decisions about passing. This is a fast-paced exercise that helps players' decision-making abilities during regular games when presented with full-court and half-court zone defenses.

63. Invasion

Purpose: To develop the concept of moving without the ball to a support position while under subtle defensive pressure.	**Number of Players:** 8 **Equipment:** 6 game spots, 1 basketball, 4 red jerseys, 4 blue jerseys **Time:** 10 to 12 minutes

1. Position six game spots to create a 20- by 20-foot grid that is divided into two halves.
2. Position four red players and two blue players on one half of the grid and two blue players on the other half.
3. The four red players try to keep the ball away from the two blue players. Each time they connect five passes in a row, they receive 1 point.
4. If the blue team steals the ball, they pass it to their teammates in the other half of the grid and then go join them.
5. Two of the red team members then go to the blue team side of the grid and are defenders.
6. Anytime a team commits a turnover, the other team starts the action with a free pass in the opposite grid. Play for 5 minutes, at which time the team with the most points is the winner.

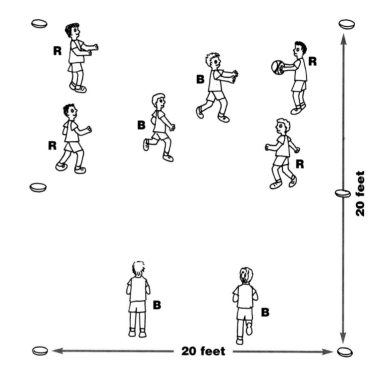

Encourage quick movement to support positions for connecting passes. Good visual scanning will help prevent two players from moving in the same space. To increase defensive pressure, add a third defender. This drill is an excellent way to teach players how to move to the open spaces available during full-court and half-court trapping defenses.

64. Sideline Passing

Purpose: To develop passing accuracy for a stationary player and collecting skills for a moving player while under gamelike defensive pressure.

Number of Players: 6
Equipment: 5 game spots, 1 basketball, 1 red jersey
Time: 8 to 10 minutes

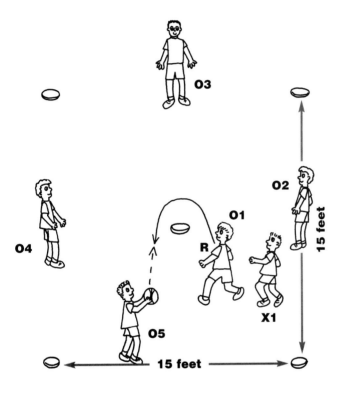

1. Position four game spots in a 15- by 15-foot grid.
2. Place a fifth game spot in the middle of the grid.
3. Position players so that one offensive player with a red jersey, Player O1, and one defender, Player X1, are in the middle of the grid, and one offensive player is on each sideline.
4. On your signal, Player O1 moves around the game spot followed by the defender. One of the sideline players, O5, has the ball and passes it to Player O1. Player O1 collects the ball, pivots while assuming a triple-threat position, makes one or two dribbles, and passes to another player on the sidelines of the grid.
5. After passing, Player O1 moves around the game spot again and repeats the action.
6. Players count how many consecutive passes can be made in 1 minute without the defender touching the ball.

This drill is excellent for helping players to develop the concept of collecting the ball, looking around, and making a decision. It helps reinforce the skill of being able to stop and stay balanced when collecting the ball under defensive pressure. Suggest to players that when they pivot under defensive pressure, they should protect the ball by tucking it back and to the side and by leading with the elbows.

65. Line Passing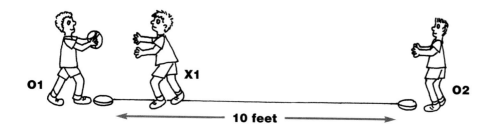

Purpose: To develop an understanding of how to create space for passing while under gamelike defensive pressure.

Number of Players: 3
Equipment: 2 game spots, 1 basketball
Time: 5 to 7 minutes

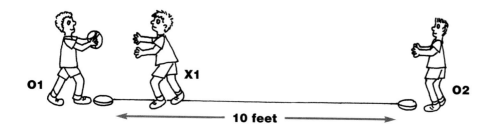

10 feet

1. Position two game spots 10 feet apart.
2. One offensive player stands behind each spot.
3. A third player, X1, assumes a closely guarded defensive position on Player O1.
4. On your whistle, Player O1 tries to bounce-pass the ball to Player O2.
5. If the pass is successful, Player X1 moves to aggressively defend Player O2.
6. If Player X1 touches the ball, she replaces the player who caused the turnover.
7. Players count the number of consecutive passes made without a defensive touch.

Players can create space for passes when they are closely guarded by using pass fakes and stepping away from the defender with the nonpivot foot. Encourage players to use a step-over move (with the nonpivot foot stepping over the pivot foot) to create extra space for passing. Do not allow players to throw passes over defenders, as this would defeat the purpose of creating space for a pass to the sides of the defender. Insist instead that players use only bounce passes.

PASSING DRILLS

66. Sideline Exchange

Purpose: To develop an understanding of how to create space for receiving a pass while under gamelike pressure.	**Number of Players:** 6 **Equipment:** 4 game spots, 1 basketball, 1 red jersey **Time:** 8 to 10 minutes

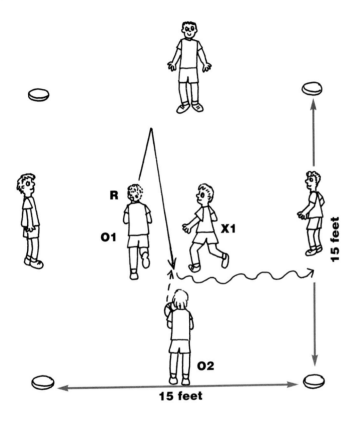

1. Position four game spots to form a 15- by 15-foot grid.
2. One offensive player, O1, wearing a red jersey, and one defensive player, X1, move to the middle of the grid.
3. One player stands on each sideline of the grid.
4. On your signal, Player O1 creates space to receive a pass from Player O2.
5. After receiving the pass, Player O1 dribbles to one of the sidelines and passes the ball to a different sideline player.
6. This sideline player replaces Player O1 and becomes the new offensive player.
7. If Player X1 touches a pass or dribble or creates a turnover, he becomes the offensive player, and the player responsible for the turnover becomes the defender.

This drill is the beginning stage of how to teach effective movement from the wing and post positions. Instruct offensive players to lean into their defender, dipping their shoulders by forcing them in one direction and then quickly moving in another direction as they break contact. Ensure that the act of leaning into the defender and moving away is not sufficiently aggressive to be called a foul.

67. Add-on Passing 👆🏀 → 👆🏀

Purpose: To pass the ball successfully between teammates when under increasing defensive pressure.

Number of Players: 12
Equipment: 1 basketball, 6 red jerseys, 6 blue jerseys
Time: 7 to 10 minutes

1. Divide players into two teams of six.
2. The blue team is positioned on one half of the court with one ball. The red team is on the sideline.
3. One member of the red team comes into the half-court as a defender.
4. The blue team tries to pass the ball between its team members, counting each successful pass. The maximum number of passes they are allowed is 10. If the defender touches the ball or the ball goes out of the half-court, the count stops.
5. Once the blue team reaches 10 passes or if they are stopped because of a violation, a second red defender goes onto the half-court. Play is repeated.
6. After each successful attempt at 10 consecutive passes or after each violation, a red defender is added.
7. Play continues until all red players are on the half-court.
8. Players then switch roles, with the red team starting on the half-court. Scores are compared to determine the winner.

The passing team is allowed one free pass before the defending team can defend. Players should be encouraged to move without the ball to create passing opportunities. As always, communication and vision will be factors in connecting passes successfully. To encourage maximum movement, have players use only bounce passes.

68. Four-Corner Passing

Purpose: To develop the concept of pass and move while under subtle defensive pressure.

Number of Players: 6
Equipment: 4 game spots, 1 basketball, 2 red jerseys
Time: 8 to 10 minutes

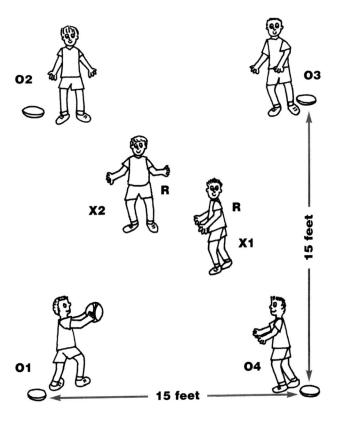

1. Position four game spots to form a 15- by 15-foot grid.
2. Place one offensive player on each corner of the grid.
3. Two defensive players wearing red jerseys are positioned in the center of the grid.
4. On your signal, the player with the ball bounce-passes the ball to another player. Each successful pass counts 1 point. If the offensive player bounce-passes between the defenders to another player, they are awarded 2 points.
5. Each time a player passes, that player must switch positions with either of the offensive players who did not receive the pass.
6. Players count score out loud. If a defender touches the ball or creates a turnover, the count starts over again. Play for 2 minutes and change defenders.

This drill helps players learn not to stand and watch after they pass. It also helps them determine where to move in relationship to other players. This concept is essential in maintaining proper floor balance when executing half-court offenses.

69. Two-Grid Passing

Purpose: To develop concepts of movement without the ball to a support position while under gamelike defensive pressure.

Number of Players: 5
Equipment: 6 game spots, 1 basketball, 2 red jerseys
Time: 8 to 10 minutes

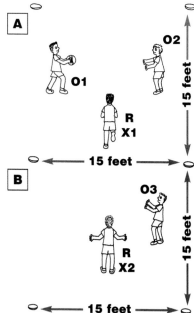

1. Position six game spots to create two 15- by 15-foot grids side by side.
2. Position two offensive players, O1 and O2, and one defensive player, X1, who is wearing a red jersey, in grid A. In grid B, place one offensive player, O3, and one defensive player, X2, who is wearing a red jersey.
3. The offensive players in grid A try to maintain possession of the ball by passing and moving in the grid. They are not allowed to dribble. When possible, they pass to the offensive player, O3, in grid B. The player from grid A who did not pass to grid B now goes to grid B and supports. Now there is a two-on-two situation in grid B.
4. The defensive player tries to touch the ball by defending the space between the players.
5. Offensive players are not allowed to throw the ball over the defender and cannot hold the ball for more then 5 seconds.
6. If the defender touches the ball, she switches roles with the offensive player who was responsible for the turnover.
7. If a 5-second violation occurs, the offensive player holding the ball becomes the defender.
8. Each time offensive players connect five passes in a row, they receive 1 point.
9. The offense has 1 minute to earn as many points as possible, then players reverse roles.

Encourage the offensive player without the ball to change speed and direction to create a space for a pass. After passing, encourage the offensive player to move to an open space at a good passing angle for her partner. The player who is being defended one-on-one should move her defender away from the grid where the two-on-one action is taking place. This will create a space for her to suddenly change directions and come to the ball. If the defender insists on staying between the offensive player and the ball, the offensive player moves her toward the two-on-one grid and then changes direction quickly in a lateral direction. This is an important exercise in the development of the type of movement needed at the wing and post positions to create space for receiving entry passes.

70. Neutral Player Passing

Purpose: To develop concepts of movement without the ball to a support position while under game-like defensive pressure.

Number of Players: 5
Equipment: 4 game spots, 1 basketball, 2 red jerseys, 2 blue jerseys, 1 yellow jersey
Time: 8 to 10 minutes

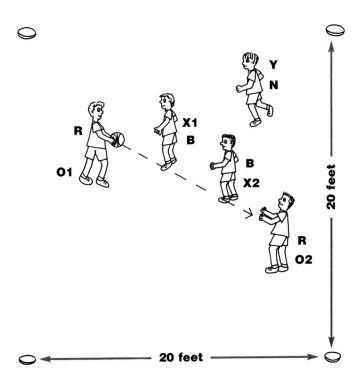

1. Position four game spots to create a 20- by 20-foot grid.
2. Position two players wearing red jerseys, O1 and O2, two players wearing blue jerseys, X1 and X2, and one neutral player wearing a yellow jersey, N, in the middle of the grid.
3. The red players start on offense and are in possession of the ball.
4. The two red players try to connect five passes in a row without the blue players touching the ball and without committing a violation, such as a 5-second violation or traveling.
5. To accomplish this, the red players may use the neutral player in the yellow jersey.
6. The blue players get the ball before the completion of the five passes if they can touch it or cause a turnover or if the red players commit a violation.
7. The blue players then try to connect five passes using the neutral player.

Encourage players to move to open spaces and communicate when their team is in possession of the ball. Good visual scanning allows players to see the neutral player. Changing direction and speed quickly helps to create spaces to receive passes. After receiving a pass, players should collect the ball, look around, and make a decision while assuming the triple-threat position.

71. End Zone Target

Purpose: To develop concepts of movement without the ball to a support position while under game-like defensive pressure.

Number of Players: 7
Equipment: 4 game spots, 1 basketball, 2 red jerseys, 2 blue jerseys, 3 yellow jerseys
Time: 8 to 10 minutes

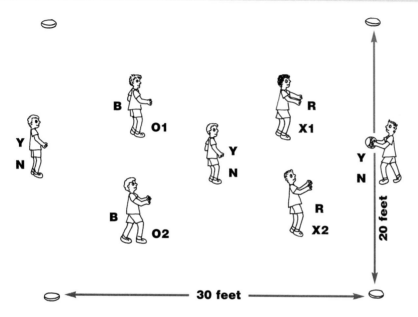

1. Position four game spots to create a 20- by 30-foot rectangle.
2. Position one neutral player wearing a yellow jersey at each end of the rectangle. They are the targets.
3. Position two players wearing blue, O1 and O2, two players wearing red, X1 and X2, and one neutral player wearing yellow inside the rectangle.

4. The blue players attempt to pass the ball to the neutral target player at one end line, to move the ball to the opposite end line by passing to each other and the neutral player, and then to pass to the other neutral target player. The neutral player inside the rectangle is not allowed to pass to target players.

5. Each time the blue players are successful in passing to both target players, they receive 1 point and maintain possession of the ball.
6. If the red players steal the ball or create a turnover, then they become the offensive team, and the blue players become the defenders.

Only bounce passes are allowed in this activity. This restriction encourages movement without the ball to open spaces. Neutral players should be used to help create open space. and to reduce some defensive pressure, allowing players to connect passes more successfully.

CHAPTER 6

Shooting Drills

There's not much in life that makes basketball players happier than scoring a basket. They love shooting in practice and games. It's important that players develop correct shooting techniques from the outset, since it's very difficult to unlearn poor habits.

Proper shooting techniques involve correct alignment of body parts and rhythmical extension of flexed arms and legs. Correct alignment begins with the toes pointing to the basket, which helps players to square their shoulders to the basket. Knees and elbows are flexed. The shooting hand is placed on the ball so that the index finger is approximately in the center of the ball. The ball rests on the fingertips, not in the palm of the hand. Cupping the hand slightly helps ensure that the fingertips do the work on release of the shot. The wrist is cocked so that the player can hold the ball in the shooting hand without dropping it. The nonshooting hand rests lightly on the side of the ball to act as a guide hand in the process of moving the ball toward release. As the ball is released, the hand continues in a follow-through motion. During the shooting process, the eyes are fixed on the basket.

Most of the poor shooting techniques I see in young players occur because they often shoot on regulation, 10-foot-high baskets. In order to generate enough force to get the ball up to the basket, they throw the ball instead of shooting it. Their bodies are not ready for 10-foot baskets. I recommend that 6- to 8-year-olds play on baskets no higher than 8 feet; 7 feet is even better. The balls they use should be smaller and lighter (you can buy these at a sporting goods store).

Even in the best of circumstances, beginning players will make mistakes. One of the most common mistakes concerns the use of force. Players should be taught to generate force for shooting by flexion and extension of the legs and arms. Very often beginning players use only their arms. They begin the shooting motion with their shooting elbow out, which helps them to rotate. I call this the "chicken elbow position." It results in the shooting hand moving across the body because of the twisting of the hips and shoulders. Instead, a rhythm should be established where arms and legs are flexed and extended together with the elbow and knee in alignment. As the shooting hand finishes, it should be pointing toward the basket.

As important as knowing how to shoot is knowing when and where to shoot. This can be accomplished by giving players countless opportunities to make decisions concerning shooting during the small-sided drills presented in this chapter. The drills are presented from least difficult to most difficult. Generally, the difficulty of the drill is determined by the amount of defensive pressure applied to the shooter, which ranges from none to subtle defense to gamelike defense. The drills also provide a range of shooting positions and situations—stationary, in motion, off the dribble, and screening.

When gamelike pressure is involved, it's often necessary for players to create space for shooting using the jab step and shot fake. The *jab step* is a technique where the player with the ball lunges forward with his nonpivot foot and tries to make the defender react by moving backward. The offensive player then brings his foot back toward his pivot foot. The defender begins to bring his foot forward to recover, but at this point the offensive player moves forward, taking a long step past the defender, who is caught off balance. Sometimes the defender overreacts to the jab step to the point that a shot can be taken.

Another method of creating individual defensive imbalance is with the *shot fake*, which involves the shooter faking a shot in an upward motion with her arms and hands. Although she raises her arms and hands, her legs stay flexed with hips lowered. As the defender rises up, often into the air, the shooter may create a space for a shot by using the dribble.

72. Wall Work

Purpose: To help develop correct shooting technique while under no defensive pressure.	**Number of Players:** 12 **Equipment:** 12 basketballs **Time:** 5 to 7 minutes

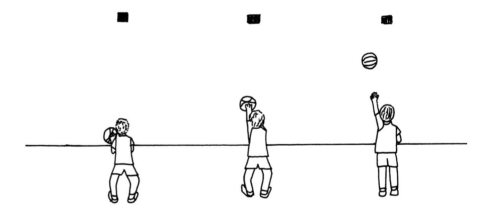

1. Tape one 2- by 2-inch square 7 feet high on the gym wall for each player.
2. Standing by the wall, the players shoot at their own square.

This simple activity allows you to observe and correct flaws in shooting mechanics. Players can work on shooting techniques without having to worry if the ball goes in the basket, and the activity allows all players to work on shooting, even when there are many players but few baskets. You should emphasize correct hand placement on the ball: hand over elbow, elbow aligned properly over knee (no "chicken elbow"), balanced feet, eyes on target, follow-through, flexion, and rhythmic extension of arms and legs.

73. Risky Rebound

Purpose: To help develop shooting accuracy while under no defensive pressure.

Number of Players: 2
Equipment: 1 basketball, 1 basket
Time: 8 to 10 minutes

1. Player O1 stands outside the 3-second lane and takes a shot.
2. If he makes the shot, the shooter gets the ball back. He returns to outside the 3-second lane and shoots again.
3. Anytime a shot is missed, Player O1 must get the rebound and shoot from wherever he rebounds the ball. If the ball rebounds out-of-bounds, the player is allowed two dribbles from the line where the ball went out-of-bounds.
4. Player O1 has 1 minute to make as many shots as he can.
5. Player O2 counts the number of shots made by Player O1. When the minute is up, players reverse roles.

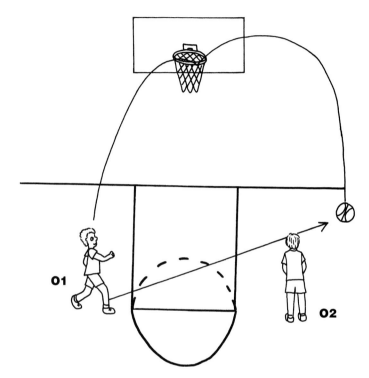

This is an excellent drill for giving shooters practice in following their shots and in rebounding the ball in good position to take a shot. No dribbling should be allowed unless the shot rebounds out-of-bounds. The game is even more fun when several players are playing at the same time and shooting at the same basket, with crazy rebounds going in several directions.

74. Lucky 7 Shooting

Purpose: To develop shooting accuracy while under no defensive pressure.

Number of Players: 2
Equipment: 1 basketball, 1 basket
Time: 8 to 10 minutes

1. Player O1 is competing against a partner who does not defend.
2. Player O1 may shoot the ball anywhere outside the 3-second lane. Player O2 rebounds.
3. Two points are earned if Player O1 makes the basket. If the shot is missed, Player O2 earns 1 point.
4. The first player to accumulate 7 points wins the game.
5. After each game, players reverse roles.

Several players may play this game at the same time. Shooting practice becomes more competitive, with players concentrating on the fundamentals of shooting because they are competing. As the players become more skilled, change the scoring system. Give the shooter only 1 point for each basket and the partner 1 point for a miss. To make the game even more challenging, the shooter earns 1 point for a basket and the partner 2 points for a miss.

75. Partner Layup

Purpose: To develop shooting technique for executing a layup while under no defensive pressure.	**Number of Players:** 2 **Equipment:** 1 game spot, 1 basketball, 1 basket **Time:** 3 to 5 minutes

1. Position one game spot at the foul line.
2. Player O1 drives to the basket from above the foul line, shoots a layup, and gets her own rebound.
3. Player O1 then passes to Player O2 and runs behind the game spot.
4. Player O2 passes to Player O1, who drives to the basket again for a layup.
5. This action continues for 1 minute, with Player O1 counting the number of successful attempts.
6. After 1 minute, players reverse roles.

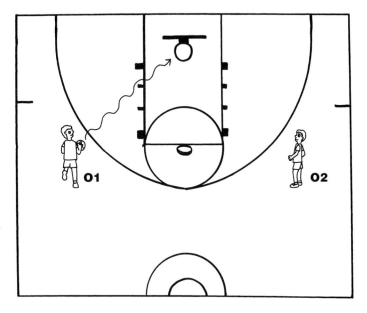

Player O1 should alternate moving around the spot on both the right and left sides. Remind your players to go hard to the basket in gamelike fashion, making sure to push off the opposite foot and to accelerate vertically as much as possible.

SHOOTING DRILLS

76. Never-Ending Layup

Purpose: To develop an understanding of correct shooting techniques when executing a layup while under no defensive pressure.

Number of Players: 12
Equipment: 4 basketballs, 2 baskets
Time: 8 to 10 minutes

1. Divide players into two teams of six.
2. Position one team so that there is a passer at each elbow of the foul line and one at the junction of the midcourt line and sideline.
3. The shooting team begins with three players under each basket.
4. On your signal, Player O1 passes to X1 (and moves down the court), who passes back, then to X2, who passes back, and then to X3, who passes back for a layup. Player O1 then goes in the opposite direction starting in O4's original position, passing to X4, X5, and X6 before finishing with a layup.
5. As soon as Player X1 passes back to O1, Player O2 passes to X1.
6. When Player X1 passes back to O2, O3 passes to X1.
7. At the same time Player O1 starts passing, Player O4 starts passing from the opposite side.
8. The action is repeated for 2 minutes, with players counting the number of successful layups.
9. After 2 minutes, players reverse roles. The winner is the team that makes the most layups.

Encourage players to drive hard to the basket in gamelike fashion. They should finish the layup by pushing off the opposite foot (for a right-handed layup, the player pushes off the left foot) in a vertical direction as much as possible. When executing the right-handed layup, the right knee is extended upward as the right arm is extended.

77. Two-Ball Shooting

Purpose: To develop proper shooting techniques while under no defensive pressure.

Number of Players: 3
Equipment: 2 basketballs, 1 basket
Time: 5 to 7 minutes

1. Position Players O1 and O2 on 3-point arc and O3 in the post.
2. Player O1 shoots and follows his shot to get the rebound.
3. Player O3 passes a second ball to Player O2 and then sprints to the 3-point arc to prepare for a shot opportunity.
4. Player O2 shoots and follows his shot to get the rebound.
5. After Player O1 rebounds his own shot, he passes to O3 and then sprints to the arc.
6. After Player O2 rebounds his own shot, he passes to O1.
7. Players repeat the action, counting the number of baskets made.

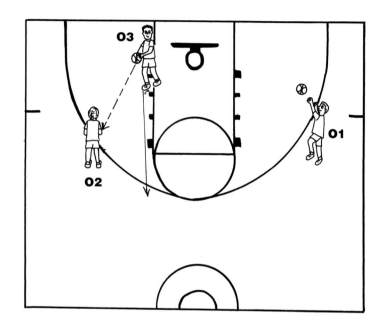

This drill offers a great opportunity for players to work on the mechanics of shooting without defensive pressure. Players should vary the action by shooting without dribbling or with one or more dribbles after a shot fake.

SHOOTING DRILLS

78. Drop-Step Shooting

Purpose: To develop the drop-step pivot move when shooting in the low-post position while under no defensive pressure.

Number of Players: 3
Equipment: 2 basketballs, 1 basket
Time: 6 to 8 minutes

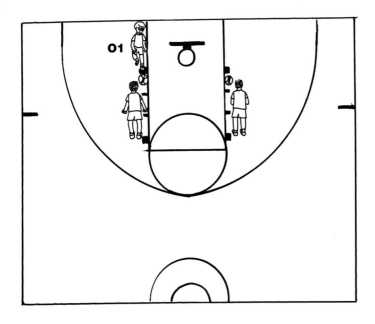

1. Place one basketball on the second block of each side of the 3-second zone.
2. Position one offensive player, O1, between one of the basketballs and the basket so that her back is to the basket.
3. Position two rebounders, one on each side of the lane by the second block.
4. On your signal, Player O1 takes a long step toward the ball, picks it up, takes a drop step, and shoots a layup.
5. Player O1 then touches the end line, quickly moves to the ball on the other side of the lane, and repeats the action.
6. The rebounder on each side of the lane has the responsibility of getting the rebound and placing the ball back on the floor by the foul line.
7. Players repeat this action for 1 minute, counting the number of layups made, and then rotate positions.

The drop step is a potent weapon for post players. Ask the shooter to step toward the ball with her right foot when she is on the right side. She then drops her left foot while pivoting on the right foot and at the same time executing one power dribble to the basket. Insist that post players go up strong to the basket using two hands on the ball.

79. Two-Team Shooting

Purpose: To develop shooting accuracy while under no defensive pressure.

Number of Players: 12

Equipment: 8 game spots, 12 basketballs, 2 baskets

Time: 8 to 10 minutes

1. Position eight game spots to make two adjoining grids, one on each side of the court.
2. Divide players into two teams.
3. Position players in grid. Each player has a basketball and a number, such as 1 through 6.
4. Players begin dribbling the balls in the grid.
5. You call out a number. The player in each grid with that number dribbles toward his basket and takes a shot.
6. If the player misses the shot, the next highest number player dribbles and shoots.
7. The first player to make the basket receives a point for his team, and the first team to reach 10 points wins.
8. If you call out a number and then say "opposite," each player has to shoot at the basket on the opposite side of the court.

This game builds players' decision-making skills concerning shooting range. The longer the shot a player can make, the better it is for his team because the first basket wins the point. But shooting long shots that sacrifice accuracy doesn't win points in this game. Players get practice at determining a good range for their shots, and this knowledge can transfer to real game situations.

SHOOTING DRILLS

80. Partner 30-Second Shooting

Purpose: To develop shooting accuracy while under no defensive pressure.

Number of Players: 2
Equipment: 1 basketball, 1 basket
Time: 6 to 8 minutes

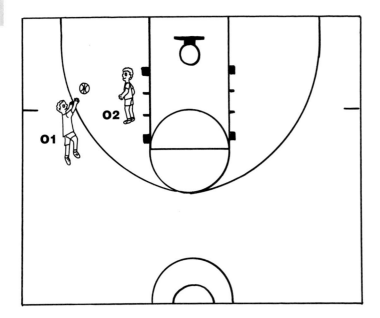

1. Position one player, O1, outside the 3-point arc with a basketball and the other player, O2, inside the 3-second lane.
2. On your signal, Player O1 shoots the ball and follows her shot while Player O2 relocates outside the 3-point arc.
3. When Player O1 collects the ball, she passes it to Player O2, who takes her shot while outside the arc.
4. This action is repeated for 1 minute.

Speed makes shooting more complicated. Players are to make as many shots as they can in a 1-minute time frame. They need to get their shots off quickly without sacrificing shooting form.

This is a great shooting activity to add a little competition to shooting practice. You may want to have more than one partner group shooting at the same time, with each group announcing its score after each successful basket. The pair of players with the most points is the winner.

81. Partner Challenge

Purpose: To develop proper shooting technique from varying distances while under no defensive pressure.	**Number of Players:** 2 **Equipment:** 5 game spots, 1 basketball, 1 basket **Time:** 8 to 10 minutes

1. Position five game spots along the 3-point arc, one each at the baseline and foul line extended on each side of the court and the fifth at the top of the key.
2. Player O1 shoots the ball from behind the 3-point arc at the game spot located nearest the baseline. Player O2 rebounds and passes the ball back to Player O1.
3. Player O1 then moves inside the 3-point arc but outside the key and shoots again.
4. Player O2 again rebounds the ball and passes it to Player O1, who drives to the basket and finishes with a layup.

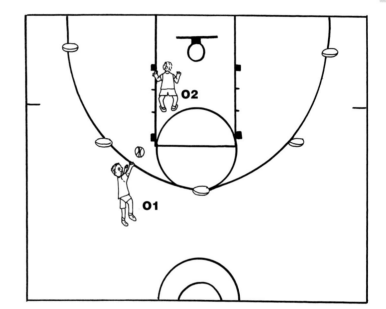

5. Player O1 repeats this action from each of the five game spots and receives 3 points for every shot made behind the three-point arc, 2 points for shots inside the arc but outside of the key, and 1 point for every layup.
6. After Player O1 finishes shooting, the players reverse roles, and Player O2 becomes the shooter.
7. The player with the highest point total wins.

   This drill develops shooting technique from varying ranges and angles. Stress the importance of correct shooting form from all ranges. If form is sacrificed for distance, then accuracy may be affected.

82. Three-Player Shooting

Purpose: To develop an understanding of the creation of open space for a shot opportunity from guard to guard position while under no defensive pressure.

Number of Players: 3
Equipment: 2 basketballs, 1 basket
Time: 8 to 10 minutes

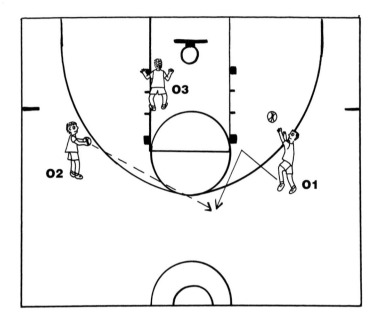

1. Position Player O1, the shooter, and Player O2, who also has a ball, on the 3-point arc.
2. Position Player O3 inside the 3-second lane.
3. Player O1 shoots the ball, executes a *V-cut*, by moving in one direction and then the opposite direction, and receives the second ball on a pass from Player O2.
4. Player O3 rebounds the shot by Player O1 and passes to Player O2.
5. Players repeat the action for 1 minute, then switch roles.
6. The shooter counts the number of shots made during the minute.

This drill offers the opportunity for numerous shots without any defensive pressure. Encourage the shooter to position himself so that he can collect the ball while "stepping in" to the shot. The shooter should select shots that are in his range and should practice shooting from places on the floor where he would normally be in game situations.

83. Guard Relocation Shooting 🏀

Purpose: To develop an understanding of the creation of open space for a shot opportunity from post to guard position while under no defensive pressure.

Number of Players: 3
Equipment: 2 basketballs, 1 basket
Time: 8 to 10 minutes

1. Position players so that Player O1 is outside the 3-point arc with a ball.
2. Players O2 and O3 assume low-post positions, and Player O3 also has a ball.
3. Player O1 passes to Player O2 and relocates to another position outside the arc.
4. Player O2 passes back to Player O1, who takes a shot.
5. Player O2 rebounds.
6. Player O3 passes to Player O1, who passes back to Player O3 and relocates.
7. Player O3 passes to Player O1 for a shot. Player O3 then rebounds.
8. Players continue action for 1 minute and then change roles.

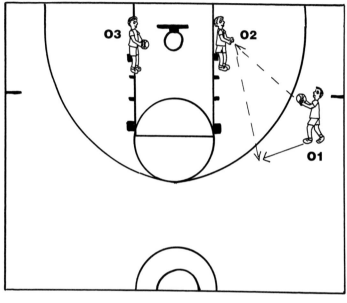

This drill is excellent for reinforcing the pass-and-move concept, where guards need to relocate after entry passes to forwards in order to create space for the forwards to pass the ball back to them. When a guard's defender double-teams the forward, then relocating to a different space away from the path of the defender is essential for the guard.

84. 20-Point Team Shooting

Purpose: To develop shooting accuracy while under no defensive pressure.

Number of Players: 12
Equipment: 2 baskets, 12 basketballs
Time: 8 to 10 minutes

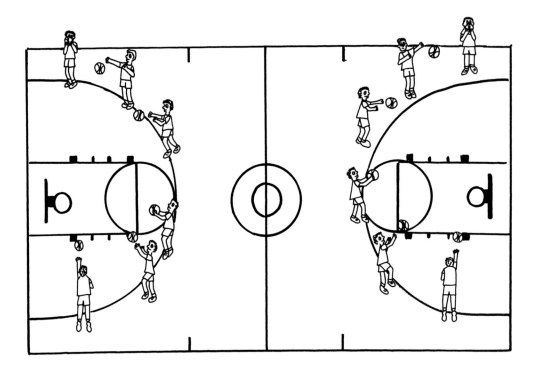

1. Divide players into two equal teams.
2. Position one team at each end of the court.
3. On your signal, the players shoot from beyond the 3-point arc.
4. Each time a basket is made, the team counts out the score, earning 1 point for each basket.
5. The first team to score 20 baskets wins.

Players will feel the need to hurry their shots because of the rush to score 20 baskets before the other team. Insist that players not sacrifice shooting form for speed. This drill helps them learn how to shoot quickly but not in a hurried fashion that leads to poor results.

85. Flyer Shooting

Purpose: To develop shooting accuracy while under subtle defensive pressure.

Number of Players: 4
Equipment: 2 basketballs, 1 basket
Time: 8 to 10 minutes

1. Position Player O1 outside the 3-point arc.
2. Player O2 has a ball and stands inside the 3-point arc approximately 5 feet from Player O1.
3. Players O3 and O4 are positioned inside the 3-second lane. Player O3 has a ball, and Player O4 is ready to rebound.
4. On your signal, Player O2 passes the ball to Player O1 and then runs at her as she attempts to shoot. After shooting, Player O1 becomes the next rebounder, replacing Player O4.

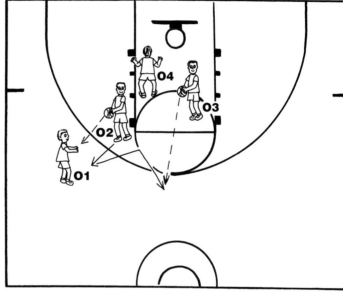

5. Player O2 executes a V-cut and receives a pass from Player O3 outside the 3-point arc. Player O3 then runs at Player O2 as she attempts to shoot.
6. Player O4, who rebounds Player O1's shot, passes to Player O3 and runs at her as she shoots.
7. Repeat several times and switch sides of the court.

Tell shooters to watch the basket while they shoot and not the defenders. When the defender runs at the shooter, she should jump with her arms and hands held high to distort the shooter's vision—almost like flying at her. Do not allow defenders to try to block shots. This drill can be made into a game by naming the first player to make five baskets the winner.

86. Three-on-Two Never-Ending Shooting

Purpose: To develop skills for determining where and when to shoot while under subtle defensive pressure.

Number of Players: 7
Equipment: 1 basketball, 2 baskets
Time: 8 to 10 minutes

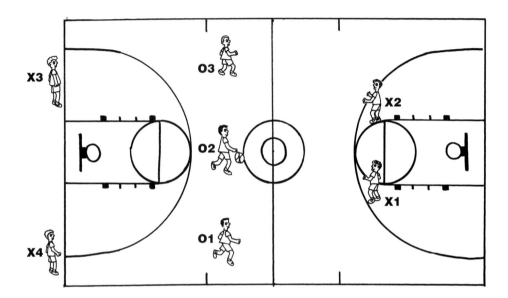

1. Position one pair of players, X3 and X4, behind one end line as waiting defensive players.
2. The offensive players, O1, O2, and O3, attack the basket at the opposite end of the court, which is defended by two players, X1 and X2.
3. The play continues until either X1 or X2 gets possession of the ball or the offensive team scores.
4. After a score or change of possession, the player who last shot the ball now teams with X1 and X2 and attacks the other basket, where the other two defenders, X3 and X4, are waiting.
5. The remaining two players of the offensive threesome go to the opposite end line and wait to be defenders.

   This activity is designed for players to make tactical decisions in a three-on-two situation. Players should consider spacing concepts, movement, shot selection, and shooting form. Encourage them to be in balance, with toes pointed toward the basket, elbow aligned and flexed properly (no "chicken elbow"), knees flexed to help generate force, eyes forward on the basket, and proper extension and follow-through of the shooting hand. This fast-paced activity is also a great conditioner.

87. One-on-One Shooting

Purpose: To develop an understanding of how to create space for a shot while under gamelike defensive pressure.

Number of Players: 4
Equipment: 1 basketball, 1 basket
Time: 8 to 10 minutes

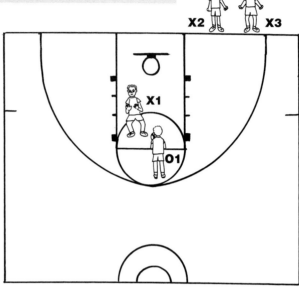

1. Position players so that two are at the foul line and two are waiting by the end line under the basket.
2. Player O1 stands with the ball behind the foul line.
3. The other player, X1, is the defender and stands in front of the foul line.
4. Player X1 asks Player O1, "Are you ready?"
5. Player O1 responds "Yes" and tries to penetrate the lane with dribbling skills and to shoot.
6. Player O1 is allowed one shot, and if this is missed, he gets one rebound and one more shot.
7. If Player O1 scores, he gets 1 point, dribbles the ball outside the 3-point arc, and tries to score on the next defender, who enters the game from the end line. He repeats this as many times as possible.
8. If the defender creates a turnover or gets a rebound, he must take the ball behind the 3-point arc and begin play against the next defender, who enters the game from the end line.
9. Offensive players who do not score or who turn the ball over must go to the end line and wait for their next turn.
10. The first player to make 6 points wins.

This is an offensive drill, so the offensive players are rewarded points for their effort. Encourage more advanced offensive players to use shot fakes, jab steps, *reverse spins* (when dribbing, a player turns his back, spins, then quickly reverses and continues dribbling in the original direction), and crossovers to create space for shots. When players cross from one side of the court to the other using the *swoop-and-go*, emphasize keeping a tight circle, which helps prevent traveling. The swoop-and-go is an offensive maneuver where the offensive player executes a shot fake, brings the ball down in a circular motion past one knee and next the other knee, and then takes a long step past the defender. Promote offensive players attacking the defender's front foot when possible. Keep the game fast-paced with small groups of four using multiple baskets.

88. Open-Space Shooting

Purpose: To develop an understanding of the creation of open space for a shot opportunity while under gamelike defensive pressure.

Number of Players: 2
Equipment: 1 basketball, 1 basket
Time: 5 to 7 minutes

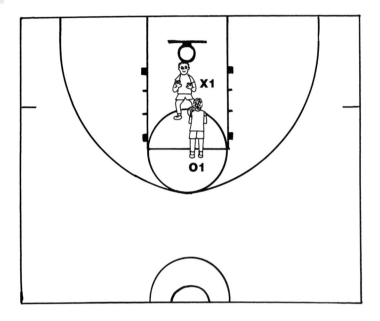

1. Position Player O1 at the foul line, being closely guarded by defender X1.
2. On your signal, Player O1 executes a shot fake and then a swoop-and-go maneuver.
3. Player O1 is allowed only two dribbles to get off a shot and then follows the shot and rebounds the ball if the shot is missed. She is allowed only one opportunity to rebound for each shot.
4. Player O1 has five opportunities to score from the foul line. Each basket counts 2 points, and each follow-up rebound and basket count 1 point.
5. After five opportunities, players switch roles.
6. Whichever player has the most points wins the game.

Emphasize that players should keep the "swoop" in a tight circle to prevent traveling and should take a long first step instead of dribbling past the defender to prevent the defender from stealing the ball. Have players think about what happens when the offensive player consistently moves one direction, or what happens when the defensive player charges too quickly at the offensive player.

89. J-Move Shooting

Purpose: To develop shooting accuracy in the post position while under gamelike defensive pressure.

Number of Players: 3
Equipment: 1 basketball, 1 basket
Time: 8 to 10 minutes

1. Position Player O1 outside the 3-point arc with a ball.
2. Player O2 is in the low-post position on the opposite side of the court from Player O1. Player O2 is guarded by Player X1.
3. On your signal, Player O2 executes a *J-move* (his path forms a J) to the opposite elbow of the foul line and receives a pass from Player O1.
4. Player O2 squares up to the basket by reverse pivoting so that his shoulders and feet face the basket, takes a shot, or performs a shot-fake, swoop-and-go move to the basket.

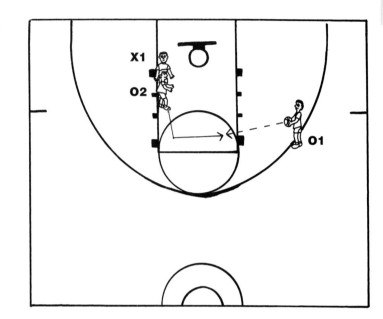

5. If the shot is missed, both players fight for rebound. If Player O2 rebounds, he shoots again. If Player X1 gets the rebound or if Player O2 makes the shot, Player X1 dribbles out beyond the 3-point arc.
6. Player O1 goes to the low-post position while Player O2 prepares to defend him. Player X1 makes the entry pass to Player O1 as he executes the J-move.
7. Players repeat the action until each player has had several opportunities to shoot.

   For the purpose of this drill, the defender must play behind the offensive player who is executing the J-move so that the offensive player can collect the ball and square up to the basket. This drill may also be used to develop *back-door moves* (where the offensive player fakes in one direction and then moves behind the defender to receive a pass from a teammate) from the baseline and *step-and-clear moves* (a post maneuver where the player steps toward the ball, collects it, and pivots toward the basket) from the low-post position.

90. Partner Spot Shooting

Purpose: To create space for a shot opportunity while under gamelike defensive pressure.	**Number of Players:** 2 **Equipment:** 5 game spots, 1 basketball, 1 basket **Time:** 8 to 10 minutes

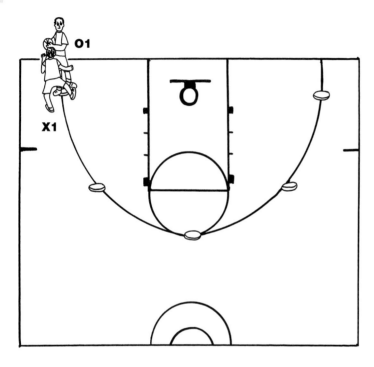

1. Position five game spots around the 3-point arc.
2. Player O1 begins at the game spot on the baseline while being guarded by Player X1.
3. Player O1 has 5 seconds to score on Player X1. Player O1 is allowed one rebound opportunity for each turn.
4. Players switch roles so that Player X1 has 5 seconds to score at the first game spot. Players then move to the remaining game spots until each player has had a turn at each spot.
5. The winner is the player with the most points; 1 point is awarded for each basket.

Suggest that players use such tactics as feinting, the jab step, and the shot fake to create open space. When they have the open space, dribbling maneuvers such as the crossover dribble and the reverse dribble should be used to upset the defender's balance. The position of the game spots should be varied for forwards to include post positions.

91. One-on-One Full-Court Shooting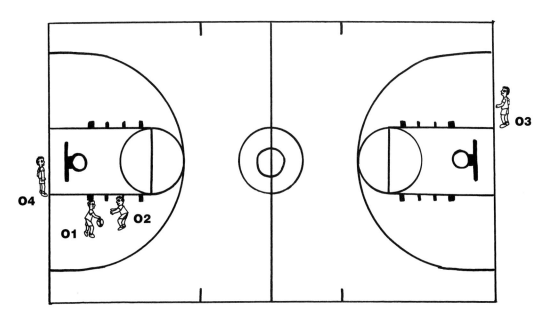

Purpose: To develop shooting accuracy while under gamelike defensive pressure.

Number of Players: 4
Equipment: 1 basketball, 2 baskets
Time: 8 to 10 minutes

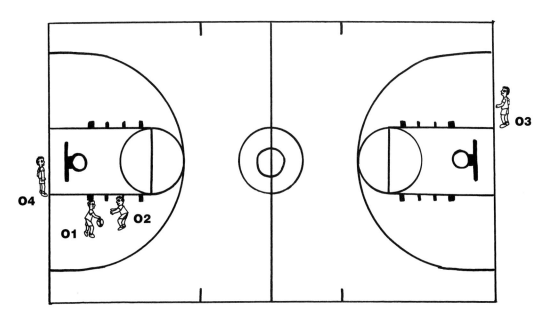

1. Position three players near one basket and one player near the other basket.
2. On your signal, Player O1 dribbles toward the opposite basket while Player O2 guards her.
3. If Player O1 scores, she becomes the new defender.
4. Player O2 then takes possession of the ball, stands behind the basket, and tries to rebound the ball to Player O3, who enters the court and is guarded by Player O1.
5. Player O3 dribbles to the opposite basket and tries to score. If successful, she becomes the new defender while Player O1 rebounds the ball to Player O4.
6. Anytime the offensive player misses the shot, she may grab the rebound and shoot again.
7. If the offensive player misses the shot and the defender gets the rebound, the defender becomes the offensive player and tries to score at the opposite basket while the player who missed the shot becomes the defender.

This drill is a great conditioner because players are running from one end of the court to the other. To reduce fatigue, you may decide to limit the running by using side baskets. Encourage players to use a variety of offensive moves that include driving to the basket and shooting from the 3-point arc.

92. Two-on-Two Full-Court Shooting

Purpose: To create open-space opportunities for shooting using screening techniques while under gamelike defensive pressure.

Number of Players: 12
Equipment: 1 basketball, 2 baskets
Time: 8 to 10 minutes

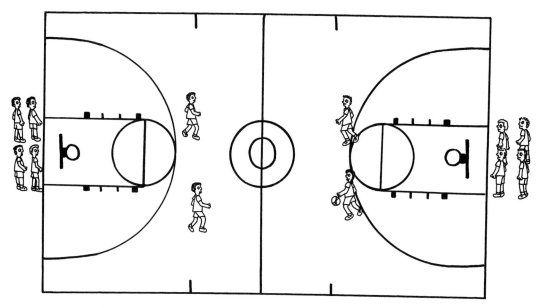

1. Position half the players in pairs behind the end line on each side of the court.
2. One pair begins moving the ball toward the basket on the opposite end line as the first pair of players from that end comes out to defend.
3. If the offensive players score, they become defenders immediately.
4. The players who were the defenders go behind their end line and wait for their next turn.
5. Two players from that end line come out to be the new offensive players and attack the basket at the opposite end line.
6. If the defenders are able to take possession of the ball by getting a rebound, forcing a turnover, or blocking a shot, they immediately become offensive players and attack the basket at the opposite end line.
7. The pair that scores 5 points first is the winner; 1 point is awarded for each basket.

This is a great activity to help build endurance while developing screening techniques. To vary the outcomes of the activity, place restrictions on players, which might include no dribbling, the use of bounce passes only, scoring only with the screen and roll, or scoring only with an outside shot off a screen.

93. Three-on-Three Half-Court Shooting

Purpose: To develop decision-making skills related to scoring while under gamelike defensive pressure.

Number of Players: 12
Equipment: 1 basketball, 1 basket
Time: 8 to 10 minutes

1. Divide players into four teams of three.
2. Two teams play three-on-three while the other two teams wait to enter the game from behind the end line under the basket.
3. As soon as one team scores, it must get to the ball, pass it outside the 3-point arc, and try to score again while the next three-person team in line enters the game.
4. The team that scores a basket stays in the game.
5. The first team to score 10 baskets wins.

You can use this activity to focus on a particular part of the game. For example, you might put a no-dribble restriction on players who are dribbling too much and not looking to get teammates involved in the action. Other variations of the game might include only shooting off screens, limiting the number of dribbles, *three-player combinations* (three players involved in an offensive play), using the give-and-go only, or requiring a specific number of passes.

CHAPTER 7

Defensive
Drills

There are two main types of defense: *player-to-player*, where defenders are assigned a player to guard, and *zone*, where defenders are assigned a space to protect. There are also more sophisticated combinations of the two. This book features elements of player-to-player defense—including vision, communication, and movement—as they relate to the two most basic rules of player-to-player defense: staying between the player you're guarding and the basket, and staying between your player and the ball. These elements are emphasized because players who understand them can easily apply them to zone defense situations.

Some of the drills involve individual defense whereas others involve multiple defenders. Drills in this chapter are designed to help improve defense against the shot, penetrating dribbles, penetrating passes, and screens.

Beginning players need to understand the concept of staying goal-side of the player they're guarding. This simply means they should stay between that player and the basket. To help them accomplish this, it's essential that solid defensive habits are formed early. Use the small-sided format presented in this chapter to have players flex their legs and extend their arms to *mirror* the ball ("reflect" or copy the offensive player's moves with the ball), prevent penetrating passes, and ensure balance. Players' weight should be distributed slightly forward and not on their heels, and their eyes should be focused on the opponent's middle-waist area. Although lateral movement was addressed in chapter 3, Space and Movement Drills, using a variety of drills (see drill 8, Feinting; drill 10, Lateral Direction; drill 13, Thirty-Second Lateral Movement; drill 14, Sideline Sliding; and drill 15, Triangle Sliding), the concept is revisited in the defensive drills by adding a player to defend.

To help teach player-to-player defense to 6- to 8-year-olds, I recommend three-on-three games. In three-on-three games players can't hide in a zone with five players. They must be responsible for playing defense, and there are fewer players to distort their vision. You can help players value defense by using small-sided games for beginning players, where players can "win" by playing defense and not have to worry about scoring baskets.

As players develop into intermediate and advanced players, more techniques and tactics are necessary because offensive players have more sophisticated skills and movements. They must blend their individual defensive skills with those of their teammates in more sophisticated team defensive schemes. Players need to develop *fronting* (the defender is between the offensive player and the basket), *swing-step* (a pivoting move used to counteract a change of direction by the offensive player), and *sliding* (moving laterally without crossing the feet) techniques. Their vision, communication, and movements must enable them to defend against screens, perform *help-and-recover moves* (assisting the defender guarding the offensive player with the ball), and *shepherd* (guide) opponents to desired spaces. They must know how to efficiently close the gap between themselves and the player they're guarding. As they progress, they cannot afford to be caught with their weight on their heels, crossing their feet, overreacting to jab steps and other offensive tactics, lifting up during shot fakes, or allowing offensive players to attack their front foot because it was in the wrong position. At an advanced level of play, such errors mean shot opportunities for the opposition, and more opportunities usually mean more points.

To help develop defensive skills, the drills in this chapter have been designed so that players learn through repetition. Drills are developed in a progression from least difficult to most difficult and from individual techniques and tactics to multiple player defense. Use these drills effectively in practice to eliminate players standing and waiting. For example, if a drill has four players involved in a grid and you have twelve players on your team, use three grids at the same time. You'll be able to rotate around to each grid to observe and instruct during teachable moments. Or if you have the luxury of having more than one coach, you may want one coach working with an individual while the other observes the grids.

94. Three-Player Sliding

Purpose: To improve reaction time while sliding.	**Number of Players:** 3 **Equipment:** 4 game spots **Time:** 3 to 5 minutes

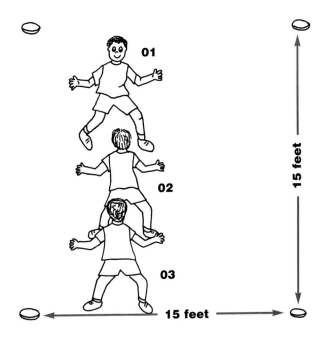

1. Position players in a 15- by 15-foot grid so that Player O1 is facing Players O2 and O3.
2. On your signal, Player O1 slides left or right, frequently changing directions as fast as he can. Players O2 and O3 must mirror this movement.
3. On your signal, Player O2 becomes the new leader.
4. On your next signal, Player O3 becomes the leader.
5. Repeat the action.

Drills on lateral movement were addressed in chapter 3. (See drill 8, Feinting; drill 10, Lateral Direction; drill 13, Thirty-Second Lateral Movement; and drill 14, Sideline Sliding.) This drill offers a different slant, because players must react to another player's movements. As you observe your players execute proper sliding techniques with legs flexed, weight slightly forward, and arms extended for balance in a small-group situation, you'll be able to correct them in a more timely manner. Small-group grid work also allows you to address the needs of varying skill levels within the team.

95. Partner Sliding

Purpose: To develop good individual defensive techniques against a dribbling offensive player.

Number of Players: 4
Equipment: 4 game spots, 2 basketballs
Time: 5 to 7 minutes

1. Position two sets of partners in a 20- by 20-foot grid so that each set occupies one corner of the grid. One partner is the defender, while the other is the offensive player and dribbles the ball.

2. One set of partners begins moving diagonally across the grid, while the other pair moves along the side of the grid to the adjacent corner.

3. As the partners move, the defenders maintain a good defensive stance, ensuring that they don't cross their feet as they move.

4. When the offensive player in each pair reaches a corner, she decides when and where to move next. If the player last moved diagonally, she must now move on a sideline. If she last moved on a sideline, she must now move diagonally. Offensive players may choose which sideline to move on, as there's no pattern for this drill.

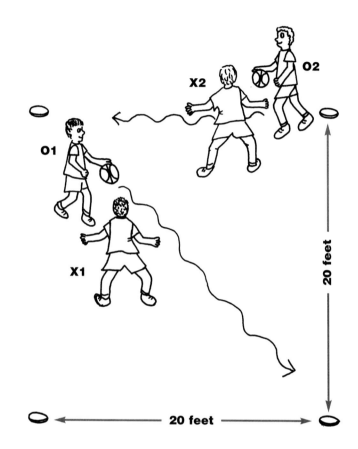

Point out that defenders need to maintain a good defensive position without "diving in" and trying to steal the ball. Players need to use good scanning techniques to avoid collisions with other partner groups. As players become more proficient, add more groups to the grid.

96. Line Work

Purpose: To develop an understanding of the defensive principle of sliding.

Number of Players: 2
Equipment: 4 game markers, 2 game spots, 1 basketball
Time: 3 to 5 minutes

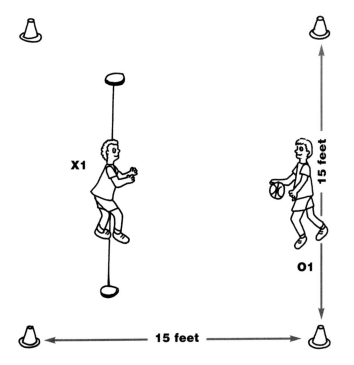

1. Position two game spots on a line in a 15- by 15-foot grid.
2. Player X1 stands on the line and takes a defensive stance.
3. Player O1 stands at one edge of the grid, facing Player X1 and the line.
4. On your signal, Player O1 attempts to dribble the ball to the other side of the grid within 5 seconds.
5. Player X1 must remain on the line to defend and may only slide laterally.
6. Player X1 receives 2 points if Player O1 does not reach the other side of the grid within 5 seconds.
7. Player O1 receives 1 point for reaching the other side.
8. The first player to reach 6 points wins the game. Then players reverse roles and repeat the action.

Encourage Player X1 to move his feet laterally using good sliding techniques: legs are flexed, weight is slightly forward, and arms are extended for good balance. Placing a time limit of 5 seconds prevents Player O1 from making too many attempts to cross the line on each turn.

97. Swing Step

Purpose: To develop good individual defensive techniques using the swing step from a stationary position.	**Number of Players:** 2 **Equipment:** 4 game spots, 1 basketball **Time:** 3 to 5 minutes

1. Position Players O1 and X1 in a 15- by 15-foot grid.
2. Player X1 stands so her front foot is forward and pointed toward Player O1's pivot foot. (If Player O1's pivot foot is her left, Player X1 puts her right foot forward.)
3. On your signal, Player O1 attacks the front foot of the defender with a spin move or crossover and takes two dribbles.
4. Player X1 reacts with a swing step.
5. Players repeat the action several times and then reverse roles.

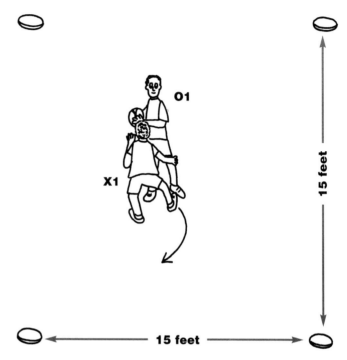

When stationary and in a good defensive stance with one foot slightly in front of the other (which foot depends on which pivot foot the ball handler is using), Player X1 is encouraging Player O1 to dribble to the side where Player X1 is best prepared to stop her. If Player O1 attacks the front foot, however, Player X1 can recover by dropping the foot she had forward while pivoting on the other foot in a backward direction. This movement, called a *swing step*, swings the defender's front foot backward, enabling her to recover and assume a solid defensive position.

98. One-on-One Defense

Purpose: To develop an understanding of individual defense techniques when defending a player with the ball.

Number of Players: 2
Equipment: 4 game spots, 1 basketball
Time: 8 to 10 minutes

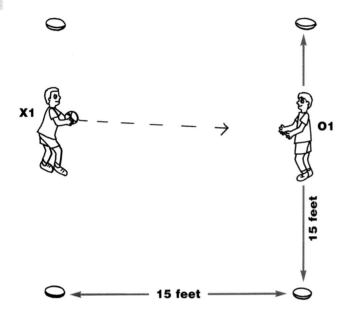

1. Position two players in a 15-by 15-foot grid formed by four game spots.
2. Player X1 passes the ball to Player O1.
3. Player O1 then tries to maintain possession of the ball without turning his back for 15 seconds, while Player X1 applies intense defensive pressure.
4. If Player X1 creates a turnover, he receives 2 points. If Player O1 maintains possession, he receives 1 point.
5. Players play a 6-point game and then reverse roles.

To get your players to value playing defense, you need to design activities where players "win" by playing defense. Since this is a defensive drill, only comment on defensive aspects of play. Encourage defenders to stay in balance, sliding quickly to deny space without "diving in" trying to steal the ball. This tactic is of particular importance when the offensive player is already in motion before the defender can close his space. Use grid work like this often so players can concentrate on movement aspects without being concerned about shooting. Insisting that defenders play with arms extended, fingertips pointed up, and palms facing opponents will help stop the "diving in" habit.

99. Shepherding 👉

Purpose: To develop an understanding of how to deny space for dribble penetration.	**Number of Players:** 2
	Equipment: 4 game spots, 1 basketball
	Time: 8 to 10 minutes

1. Position two players in a 15-by 15-foot grid.

2. Player X1 passes the ball to Player O1 and immediately begins to close the space between the two by making a slightly bended run, forcing Player O1 to go to the left side of the grid.

3. Player X1 shepherds Player O1 to the player's left side, not allowing her to touch the sideline to Player O1's right.

4. Players repeat the action several times, changing the direction in which Player X1 forces Player O1 to move.

5. Players reverse roles and play again.

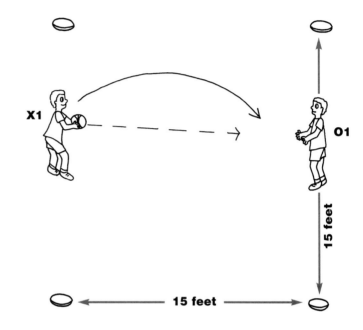

Shepherding is a term used to describe the guiding of a player in the direction the defensive player wants her to go. The defender must close the distance between the offensive player and the defender as fast as she can, making sure to remain in a good defensive stance and in balance. If the defender wants the offensive player to move to the left, she should make a slight bending run to the right of the player. The defender should have her left foot in front of her right, staying on the dribbler's right side. This position invites the player to dribble to the left. Such a defensive maneuver is important in defensive schemes using trapping along the sideline and baseline.

DEFENSIVE DRILLS

100. Denying Penetration

Purpose: To develop individual defense moves to deny dribble penetration.	**Number of Players:** 2 **Equipment:** 4 game spots, 1 basketball **Time:** 8 to 10 minutes

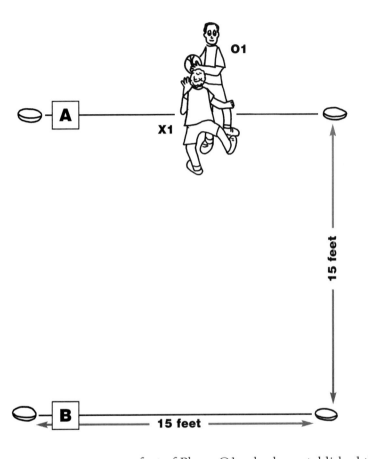

1. Position two players in a 15-by 15-foot grid.
2. Player O1 has the ball on the sideline in a triple-threat position.
3. Player X1 takes a defensive stance.
4. Player O1 uses such moves as the jab step, reverse dribble, and crossover to try to create space so that he can move from sideline A to sideline B without turning his back. If he is successful, he earns 1 point.
5. Player X1 receives 2 points if he can create a turnover and prevent Player O1 from penetrating with the dribble.
6. Players play a 6-point game and then reverse roles.

Make certain that Player X1 begins with his right foot slightly more forward than his left, aligned and pointing at the pivot foot of Player O1, who has established the left foot as his pivot foot. Encourage Player X1 not to overreact to the jab step because he is already in good defensive position if Player O1 decides to move in that direction. If Player O1 should successfully use a crossover and change direction, Player X1 should adjust by using the swing step. This is a defensive drill, so Player X1 is rewarded for his efforts with a higher point value.

101. Partner Denying Penetration

<table>
<tr><td>Purpose: To develop the concept of denying dribble penetration.</td><td>Number of Players: 4
Equipment: 1 basketball, 1 basket
Time: 8 to 10 minutes</td></tr>
</table>

1. Position players on a half-court so that two offensive players occupy the wing positions and two players, one offensive and the other defensive, are at the top of the key.
2. On your signal, Player O1 is given 5 seconds to create enough space for a shot while being defended by Player X1. Player O1 must begin with a shot fake.
3. After Player O1 takes a shot, Players X1 and O1 try to position themselves for the rebound and outlet pass and then assume wing positions.

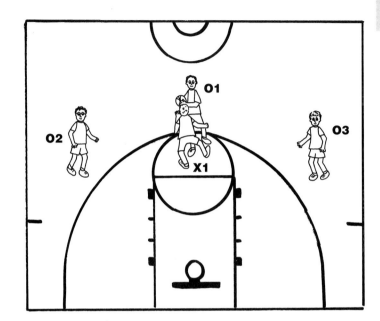

4. Whichever side the rebound goes to dictates where the outlet pass is made. If the ball goes to Player O3's side, she receives the outlet pass, dribbles to the top of the key, and repeats the previous action while being defended by Player number 4 (shown as O2 in the illustration because if the ball is rebounded on her side, she becomes the offensive player and Player O3 becomes the defensive player).

Encourage the defender to stay down on the shot fake, raising her arm to distort the offensive player's vision. Emphasize maintaining balance and movement of feet by sliding instead of placing hands on the opponent. If some defenders continue hand-checking, which is a violation, make them hold a towel behind their back while on defense. A variation for the advanced group would have them using Players O2 and O3 to create give-and-go scoring opportunities.

DEFENSIVE DRILLS

102. Denying Penetrating Passes

Purpose: To deny space for penetrating passes.

Number of Players: 7
Equipment: 4 game spots, 1 basketball
Time: 8 to 10 minutes

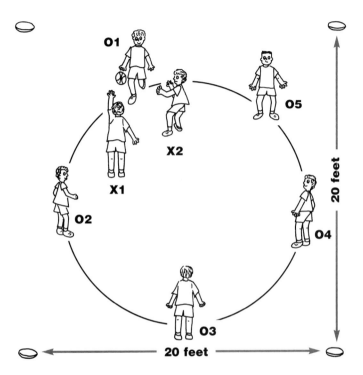

1. Position five offensive players in a circle formation inside a 20- by 20-foot grid.
2. Place two defenders inside the circle. One attacks the ball; the other slides in the passing lane.
3. On your signal, the offensive players pass the ball around the circle.
4. If a defender can touch the ball or create a turnover, he replaces the player guilty of the infraction, and the offensive player becomes a defender.

As the defender approaches the player with the ball, he should do so at an angle that helps to shut down a passing lane. The second defender positions himself between the other passing lanes, hoping to get a touch on the ball when it is passed. The defense tries to shift quickly enough to create a turnover. To make the activity more challenging, include a restriction that offensive players can't pass to players next to them.

103. Fronting in Post Position 👉 → 👉

> **Purpose:** To develop an understanding of fronting in the post area.
>
> **Number of Players:** 5
> **Equipment:** 1 basketball, 1 basket
> **Time:** 8 to 10 minutes

1. Position three players, O1, O2, and O3, around the 3-point arc.
2. Position Players O4 and X1 in the post position.
3. On your signal, Players O1, O2, and O3 pass the ball to create a space to make an entry pass to the post player, Player O4. After each pass on the arc, the offensive player holds the ball for 2 seconds.
4. Player X1 must continue to move her position in front of Player O4 to deny her the pass.
5. Players repeat the action for 1 minute and reverse roles.

Post players are sometimes satisfied to stand behind the player they're guarding or lazily place one hand around her and let the offensive player collect the ball. Usually these types of players end up in foul trouble trying to block shots. To discourage such play, emphasize to the defensive post player the importance of foot work in establishing good position in front of their player. Any attempt to lob the ball over the defender should be discouraged in this drill because there is no weak-side defender to help.

104. Defensive Communication

Purpose: To improve player-to-player defensive communication between teammates.

Number of Players: 6
Equipment: 4 game spots, 3 red jerseys, 3 blue jerseys
Time: 3 to 5 minutes

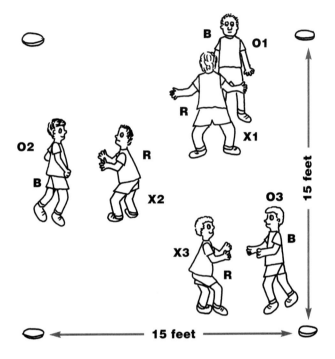

1. Position three sets of partners in a 15- by 15-foot grid.
2. Designate one color of jersey, let's say the red team, to be defense.
3. On your signal, the players on the blue team begin to move in the grid while being guarded by the red team.
4. On the next signal, each defender must find a new player to defend.
5. This action is repeated several times; then the teams reverse roles.

While defenders are switching defensive assignments, it is important that they communicate which player they are guarding. It's possible that if two defenders switch with each other, the third defender will still have the same player. The three defenders must continue talking and switching until each player has a new player to guard. As players become more proficient at this drill, add more players until there is a five-on-five situation.

105. Pick-up Defense

Purpose: To develop good defensive communication between teammates.

Number of Players: 12
Equipment: 4 game spots, 6 basketballs
Time: 3 to 5 minutes

1. Position players with partners in a 20- by 20-foot grid in a scattered formation.
2. One player in each pair dribbles the ball while the partners assume a defensive stance and slide with them.
3. On your signal, the dribbler stops dribbling and holds the ball.
4. The defensive player reacts by shouting "ball, ball, ball" as he assumes a more tightly defensive stance.
5. Players repeat several times and then reverse roles.

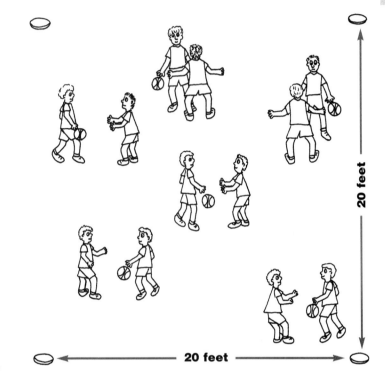

20 feet

20 feet

As the offensive player "picks up" his dribble, the defender should close the space between the two players as quickly as possible. He should mirror the ball with his hands to help prevent a shot or penetrating pass. By communicating "ball, ball, ball" to his teammates, the player is letting them know they don't have to worry about dribble penetration. In the intermediate and advanced stages, defensive players would then assume a deny position to prevent a pass to the player they're guarding.

DEFENSIVE DRILLS

106. Partner 30-Second Defense

Purpose: To develop good defensive communication between teammates.

Number of Players: 4
Equipment: 4 game spots, 1 basketball
Time: 8 to 10 minutes

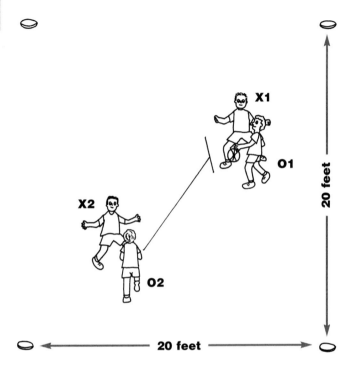

20 feet

20 feet

1. Position four players, two defensive and two offensive, in a 20- by 20-foot grid.

2. On your signal, the offensive players, O1 and O2, try to keep possession of the ball for 30 seconds using dribbling, passing, and screening skills. If they retain control, they receive 1 point.

3. The defensive players, X1 and X2, try to gain possession of the ball by creating a turnover, perhaps due to a 5-second violation, bad pass, or double dribble. If they gain control, they receive 2 points.

4. Players continue the action for 1 minute and then reverse roles.

Communication is the key to good defensive performance. Encourage players to give their partners constant information that will be helpful. Calling out where screens are located, saying "ball, ball, ball" when the dribbler has picked up the dribble, and giving direction on how to guard against screens—such as get through, switch, or hedge—are all important to the defending team's success.

107. Help and Recover 👉 → 👉

Purpose: To develop the concept of help and recover to prevent dribble penetration.

Number of Players: 4
Equipment: 4 game spots, 1 basketball
Time: 8 to 10 minutes

1. Position four players, two offensive and two defensive, in a 20- by 20-foot grid.
2. On your signal, Players O1 and O2 try to move the ball from sideline A to sideline B within 10 seconds by passing and dribbling. If successful, they earn 1 point.
3. The defense is in a help-and-recover position to deny penetration. If they are successful in stopping the offense from penetrating to the opposite side of the grid, they receive 2 points.
4. Players continue the action for 1 minute and then reverse roles.

   This is a fast-paced activity that requires the defense to make quick adjustments to offensive tactics. Emphasize that when playing in a help-and-recover position, the defender on the ball tries to shepherd the player she's guarding toward her defensive partner, who should be slightly behind and at an angle to her partner on the ball. Spacing is crucial: the off-the-ball defender must be in position to slide and help prevent the dribble penetration but must also be ready to defend against a pass to the player she's guarding.

108. Point-to-Wing Help and Recover

Purpose: To develop communication during help-and-recover defensive tactics.	**Number of Players:** 4 **Equipment:** 1 basketball **Time:** 3 to 5 minutes

1. Position two offensive players so that Player O1 is at the point position and Player O2 is on a wing. Player O1 starts with the ball.
2. Position two defenders, Players X1 and X2, so that the one on the ball is guarding closely and the other is in a help position.
3. On your signal, Players O1 and O2 begin passing the ball.
4. Each time the ball is passed from Player O1 to Player O2 and back, the defenders must react and assume the correct defensive positioning.
5. After 1 minute, players reverse roles.

As the ball is passed from Player O1 to O2, Player X2 must recover from a position where he dropped off Player O1 and moved several feet toward the foul line in a help position to a position where he is closely guarding his player. Simultaneously, Player X1 moves to a help position by dropping down to the foul line to "help" prevent dribble penetration to the middle. Each time a defender slides to a help position, he should call out the word "help" to his partner, giving notice that he is there if needed.

109. Step-Over Defense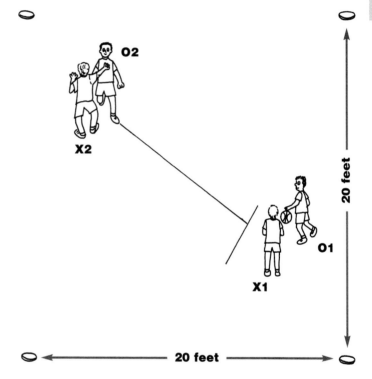

Purpose: To develop vision and communication for the step-over move to prevent being screened.

Number of Players: 4
Equipment: 4 game spots, 1 basketball
Time: 8 to 10 minutes

1. Position two offensive and two defensive players in a 20- by 20-foot grid formed by four game spots.
2. On your signal, Player O2 sets a *screen* (blocks the defender's pathway) on Player X1.
3. If the screen is successful and the defenders switch, the offense receives 1 point.
4. If the defenders communicate and Player X1 steps over the screen and stays with her player, they receive 2 points.
5. Players play a 6-point game and then reverse roles.

Placing these players in a grid without a basket removes the distraction of shooting and scoring. It allows them to concentrate on setting solid screens and to avoid being screened defensively. If you value solid player-to-player defense without switching players, there must be opportunities for players to become familiar with this type of defense. The drill gives players a chance to win a small-sided game with a strong defensive performance. As a variation, require the defenders to hedge the dribbler or move through the screen (actually between the screener and her defender) during the next practice session.

Screening is used by the offense to create space. Drills 109 and 110 will help your players defend against screens. To learn more about the technique of screening, see chapter 8, Screening.

110. No Switching

Purpose: To develop vision and communication skills between defenders while being screened.

Number of Players: 4
Equipment: 1 basketball, 1 basket
Time: 8 to 10 minutes

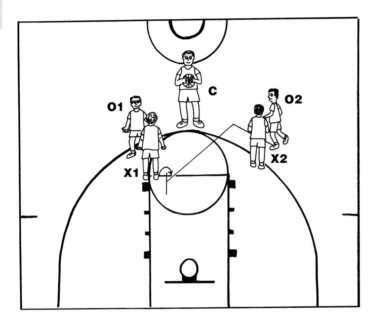

1. Position two offensive players, O1 and O2, and two defensive players, X1 and X2, on one half of the court.
2. You or an assistant are positioned at the top of the key (C). Hold the ball until an open space is created, then pass it to the open player.
3. Players O1 and O2 move around, screening and re-screening in an attempt to create an open space to collect the ball and finish to the basket.
4. The offensive team earns 1 point each time they make the defensive team switch defensive assignments.
5. Players repeat the action several times and then reverse roles.

Offensive players should be encouraged to move at different angles to the ball when screening. This provides different opportunities for the defenders to step over, slide through, and hedge on screens instead of switching the players they are guarding. Emphasize that defenders should use good peripheral vision and communication to prevent being screened, which may lead to switching assignments. When switching occurs, mismatches in height, speed, quickness, and ball handling often result. Switching is sometimes unavoidable, but it's often the lazy man's way of playing defense. Good communication and vision can often prevent it.

Screening is used by the offense to create space. Drills 109 and 110 will help your players defend against screens. To learn more about the technique of screening, see chapter 8, Screening.

Screening Drills

One of the most difficult tasks you'll encounter as a coach is helping players understand how to create opportunities for dribbling, passing, and shooting in tightly defended spaces. This is so difficult because it involves not only the player with the ball but the supporting players as well. You can make the task somewhat easier by instilling in your supporting players a mind-set where they all ask themselves the same question: Where can I go to help someone else get the ball? This thinking is completely opposite from traditional thinking by players without the ball who ask: Where can I go and get the ball? Players asking themselves where to go to help someone else get the ball will find the answer involves screening.

Screening is a technique of blocking the path of a defender who is sometimes in a stationary but most often in a moving position. The idea is to block the defender so the offensive teammate may have space to dribble, pass, or shoot when in possession of the ball. When the teammate is not in possession of the ball, the screen is used to block the defender so that the teammate has space to receive the ball.

When teaching screening techniques, it's important to identify the role of the screener (the one who sets the screen) and the player whose defender is being screened. The screener must communicate to his teammate that he is coming to set the screen. Some coaches like players to use hand signals to accomplish this, whereas others prefer a verbal method of calling out the name of the player whose defender will be screened. As the screener approaches the defender, he must decide at which angle to set the screen. The angle is determined by the position of the ball. Generally, I like telling my players that the correct screening angle should be one where the screener is facing one of the four corners of the half-court. A visual aid like this helps to simplify angles, especially for younger players.

As the screen is set, the screener should assume a wide base of support with his feet. His legs should be slightly bent. If he is too erect, he can be pushed aside too easily. The screener should keep his arms folded against his chest to protect himself if the defender runs into him (this is also a good protective move for girls). For boys, some coaches prefer them to keep their arms down with hands protecting the groin area.

The role of the player whose defender is being screened is significant in the success of the screen. The most important thing he has to do is wait for the screener to get in good position. Very often, particularly with young players, the urge to begin moving past the offensive player creates a situation where the screener is moving into a moving defender. Such a move, of course, is a moving-screen foul on the screener.

After the screener arrives to screen the defender, the offensive player whose player is being screened should "set up" the defender by moving in the opposite direction of the screener. I like to teach young players to use a *V-cut*. An example of the V-cut might involve one foot moving forward to the left. As the defender begins to move in that direction, the weight is shifted back to the right foot stepping forward past the screen. As the offensive teammate goes past the screen, he should move so close to it that he actually brushes shoulders with his teammate. This will prevent the defender from sliding through the space between the two players.

There are basically two opportunities for screening: screening for someone who has the ball and screening for someone who doesn't. Some of the most effective screens are done on those players away from the ball, because defenders are often looking at the ball and not watching for screeners.

I recommend when teaching screening that you use a sequence that begins with two offensive players and one defender. As players become more proficient, add players sequentially—going to two-on-two, three-on-three, four-on-four—until you've advanced to the five-on-five model. Use grids during the teaching of screens and challenge your players to keep possession of the ball, go in a particular direction, or finish by scoring. Vary screening drills to include, for example, no shooting, shooting of screens with no dribble, or finishing with a screen and roll (see drill 114, Screen and Roll). Do not hurry the process of teaching screening by adding too many players too soon. Insist that the players execute screening fundamentals properly, because they are the foundation for success in any offensive scheme.

111. Pass and Screen Away

Purpose: To develop an understanding of the concept of pass and screen away.	**Number of Players:** 3 **Equipment:** 4 game spots, 1 basketball **Time:** 5 to 7 minutes

1. Position three players, one each on three sides of a 15- by 15-foot grid formed by four game spots.
2. Player O1 passes to Player O2 and moves to set an imaginary screen for Player O3, who comes to the ball in the position where Player O1 started.
3. Player O3 collects the ball and passes it to Player O1; then he sets the screen for Player O2.
4. Players repeat the action.

This is the beginning of teaching three-player combinations. It helps to reinforce the idea that players don't always set screens on the ball. Insist that players demonstrate good communication (calling out the names of players for screens), show patience (waiting for the screener to set the screen), and exaggerate the V-cut in setting up the imaginary defender.

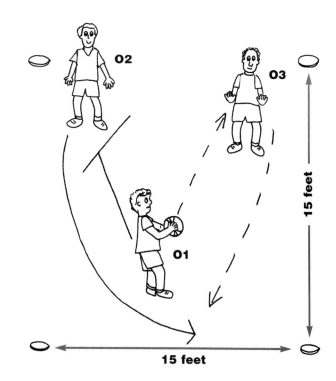

112. Ball Screen

Purpose: To develop the concept of screening on the ball.

Number of Players: 4
Equipment: 4 game spots, 1 basketball
Time: 8 to 10 minutes

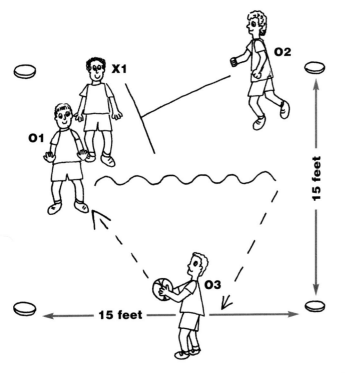

1. Position two offensive players, O1 and O2, in a 15- by 15-foot grid with one defensive player, X1.
2. Position a third offensive player, O3, outside the grid with the ball.
3. Player O3 begins the action by slapping the ball. Players O1 and O2 move forward, backward, diagonally, or laterally in relation to each other to create a space to receive a pass from Player O3. Player X1 puts as much defensive pressure on Players O1 and O2 as possible, but he may not guard Player O3.
4. Player X1 must guard whichever player receives a pass from Player O3.
5. If Player O1 receives the pass, Player O2 must set a screen on Player X1 so that Player O1 may dribble to open space and pass the ball back to Player O3.
6. Players repeat the action.

   This drill is critical in helping to develop player movement in relationship to the movement of other players. Players must constantly be aware of where other players are located by using good scanning techniques and must adjust their spacing accordingly. Encourage the player receiving the ball to collect it and look for the screen before dribbling. Collecting and looking are essential steps in the process of play. As players are engaged in the second part of the process, looking, they should assume the triple-threat position.

113. Screen and Dribble

Purpose: To develop the use of the screening concept for dribbling to open space.	**Number of Players:** 4 **Equipment:** 4 game spots, 1 basketball **Time:** 8 to 10 minutes

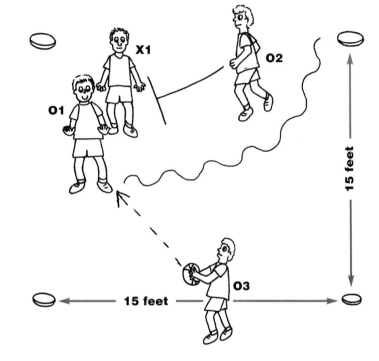

1. Position two offensive players, O1 and O2, in a 15- by 15-foot grid with one defensive player, X1.
2. Position a third offensive player, O3, outside the grid with the ball.
3. Player O3 begins by slapping the ball. Players O1 and O2 move to create space to receive the ball.
4. Player X1 must defend Player O1, who receives the pass from Player O3 and assumes a triple-threat position.
5. Player O2, who did not receive the ball, must set a screen on Player X1.
6. Player O1, who did receive the ball, must use the screen to create space to dribble to the end line opposite the passer.
7. Player O1 then becomes the passer; Player O3 steps in as an offensive player, and action is repeated.

Player O1 must collect the pass and look for the screen before dribbling. Encourage Player O1 to dribble past the screen so closely that she actually brushes against her offensive partner who set screen. Player O1 should "set up" the defensive player by using the V-cut.

114. Screen and Roll

Purpose: To develop the concept of screen and roll while defenders switch players they're guarding.

Number of Players: 8
Equipment: 4 game spots, 1 basketball
Time: 8 to 10 minutes

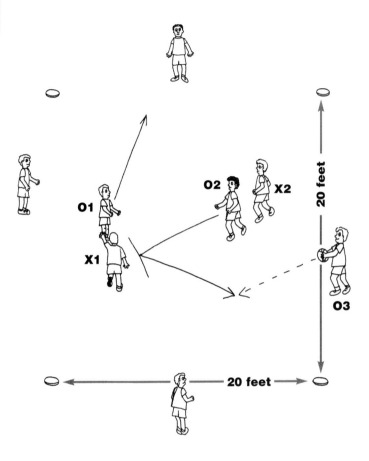

1. Position two offensive players, O1 and O2, and two defensive players, X1 and X2, in a 20- by 20-foot grid with one additional player on each side of the grid used as a passer. Player O3 has the ball.
2. Player O2 sets a screen on Player X1.
3. Player O1 moves off the screen. As Player O1 moves, Player X2 switches and now guards Player O1.
4. Player O2 then rolls to the ball to receive a pass from Player O3.
5. Player O2 passes to a different player outside the grid.
6. The action is repeated.

This drill provides hundreds of screen-and-roll opportunities using a grid. This technique is an important part of player development. The drill allows players to focus on screening and rolling properly while keeping possession of the ball, because they don't need to be concerned about scoring. When rolling to the ball, Player O2 should pivot on the foot that is closest to the defender and use his forearm to push away slightly and break contact between the two players. This action ensures that the defender is behind the offensive player and not between the player and the ball. Player O2 knows he will be the primary target for the pass because, if the defense switches, the person who sets the screen is in the best position to go to the ball.

115. Floor Spacing for Screening

Purpose: To develop proper floor spacing for screening players without shooting.

Number of Players: 6
Equipment: 1 basketball
Time: 8 to 10 minutes

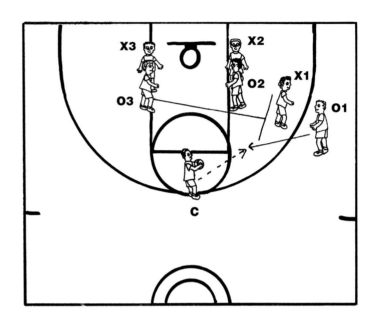

1. Position players on the half-court so that they assume the roles of wing and post players. You (or an assistant coach) stand at the point position with the ball (C).
2. Players move freely while setting screens at an angle that enables another player to receive a pass or that creates a space for movement, allowing a player to screen for another player.
3. No shots are taken during this drill.
4. Players repeat the action for 2 minutes and then reverse roles.

After players have had the opportunity to practice and develop screening techniques in small-group grid work, they should be given the opportunity to screen using more players. This should be done using the half-court to allow players to visualize the spacing necessary for proper floor balance.

Emphasize to your players that the key to good offensive movement is having the correct philosophy: go to the appropriate place to set a screen that allows somebody else to get the ball. When they can internalize this philosophy, they'll stop standing around waiting for someone to bring them the ball.

As a variation and to achieve more floor balance, increase the number of players to four-on-four plus the coach and then five-on-five.

116. Screen and Shoot

Purpose: To develop the concept of creating space for shooting using screens.

Number of Players: 5
Equipment: 1 basketball
Time: 8 to 10 minutes

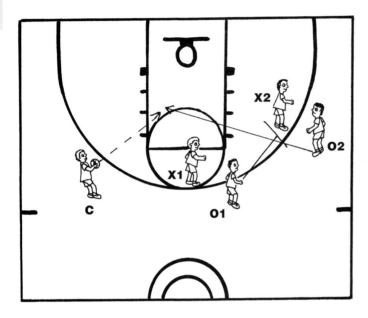

1. Position one offensive player, O1, and one defensive player, X1, at the top of the key.
2. Position one offensive player, O2, and one defensive player, X2, on the wing.
3. Player O2 does a V-cut, moving toward the basket and then quickly back to the wing.
4. Player O1 passes the ball to you or your assistant, who is on the opposite wing. (You can control the tempo of the drill this way, but another player could fill in here.)
5. Player O1 sets a screen on Player X2.
6. Player O2 cuts off the screen, receives the pass from you, and shoots.
7. Players repeat the action several times before reversing roles.

Don't allow defenders to switch during this drill. Having Player O1 drop below Player X2 and come back to screen helps ensure a good angle for Player O2 to go to the basket. Run this drill from both sides of the court so that players develop right-handed and left-handed finishing skills. As a variation of this drill, allow defenders to switch, in which case Player O1 will roll to the basket to receive a pass from you.

117. Low-Post Screening

Purpose: To develop an understanding of screening away from the ball in the post position.	**Number of Players:** 7 **Equipment:** 1 basketball, 2 red jerseys **Time:** 8 to 10 minutes

1. Position two offensive players, O4 and O5, in the low-post position.
2. Position two defensive players with red jerseys, X1 and X2, in the post position defending the offensive players.
3. Three passers, Players O1, O2, and O3, are positioned on the 3-point arc.
4. Either Player O4 or O5 moves away from the ball to screen for her post partner according to where the ball is passed. For example, if Player O1 passes to O2, Player O4 moves away from the ball and sets a screen on Player O5's defender.

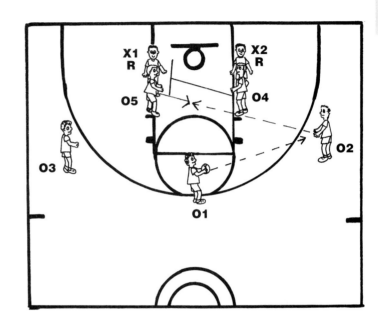

5. Player O5 moves off the screen to the open space toward the ball, where she receives a pass from Player O2 and finishes by going to the basket or shooting in from post area.

   Encourage post players who are going to set the screen to call out the name of the player whose defender they are going to screen, to screen using at least a shoulder-width stance (preferably a little wider for good stability), to use their arms to protect their chest from the opponent's elbows, and to screen at the proper angle in relation to the ball. As the ball is passed between Players O1, O2, and O3, post players should vary their positions so they are both high (by the foul line), both low (near the basket), or one high and one low to create a variety of screening angles.

Rebounding Drills

Even the best basketball teams miss more than half of their shots. That's why rebounding is one of the most important elements of basketball. It allows the team to keep possession of the ball for another shot attempt. It also lets teams regain possession of the ball, which denies the opponent another chance to score. Although size and strength are two components of a player's ability to rebound, good instincts and proper techniques are also contributors.

Defensive players generally have the advantage in rebounding because they are often goal-side of the player they're guarding. Defensive rebounding techniques involve closing the space between the defender and her player. The defender should step toward the player she's guarding and pivot in the same motion while making contact. As the defender pivots, she should maintain a low center of gravity by flexing her knees and lowering her hips. This stance is much sturdier than standing erect. Extension of the arms slightly helps to increase the amount of space the defender can seal off. One of the biggest mistakes defensive rebounders make is watching the ball after it is shot instead of watching their player, making contact, and then going for the ball.

Rebounding is difficult for the offensive player because the defender has the advantage of being goal-side. What has helped offensive rebounding in recent years is the increased number of long rebounds away from the basket because of the 3-point shot.

The offensive rebounder is often able to get only one hand on the ball and an opportunity to tip the ball away from defenders because of their goal-side position. To improve their positioning, offensive players can use a *roll*, or *reverse roll*. To execute this technique, the offensive player pivots and rolls away from the defender as the defender steps in and pivots, making contact in an effort to establish rebounding position. If the defender reacts quickly and slides to continue to block out, the offensive player quickly changes direction with a reverse roll. The offensive rebounder should always have the mind-set that she wants to get to a neutral position as quickly as possible. She wants to be in constant motion so she doesn't become an easy target for block outs. If the defender is holding her out, she should rotate her arm over top of the defender's arm by extending her arms and pulling down and away as in a swimming motion. As this motion is being completed, she steps over the defender's leg that is closest to her. Now the offensive player has the rebounding advantage.

Rebounding drills should be a part of every practice. I have often had five-on-five scrimmages and kept score, not by points, but by rebounds. If offensive rebounds are a particular problem for your team, play five-on-five and only reward points for offensive rebounds.

The drills in this chapter help develop vertical jumping ability and quickness as well as offensive and defensive techniques. They involve both one-on-one and multiple-player situations.

REBOUNDING DRILLS

118. Partner Rebounding

Purpose: To develop rebounding techniques without shooting.

Number of Players: 12
Equipment: 6 basketballs
Time: 3 to 5 minutes

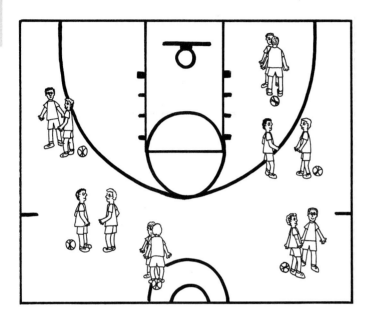

1. Position players with partners facing each other in a scattered formation.
2. One partner is the offensive player, and the other is the defender.
3. Place a ball on the floor behind the defender.
4. On your signal, the defender uses good rebounding techniques to block out the offensive player and keep her away from the ball for 10 seconds.
5. After 10 seconds, players reverse roles.

Teaching players how to initiate and maintain contact is the essence of rebounding technique. Instruct players to step toward their partners and pivot into them to make contact and close the amount of space between them. Encourage players to flex their legs and keep their hips lowered to form a strong base of support. Closing the space and creating contact will make it more difficult for the offensive player to change directions. Even though the defender cannot see the offensive player after stepping in and pivoting because her back is turned, she can feel the offensive player because of the contact.

119. Pass-and-Shoot Rebounding

Purpose: To develop defensive rebounding techniques.

Number of Players: 5
Equipment: 1 basketball, 1 basket, 1 red jersey
Time: 8 to 10 minutes

1. Position Players O1, O2, and O3 outside the 3-point arc.
2. Position Players O4 and X1, who is wearing a red jersey, in the post position.
3. Players O1, O2, and O3 pass the ball around the perimeter while Player O4 is defended by Player X1.
4. After three passes have been made, whoever is holding the ball takes a shot from outside the arc.
5. Player X1 steps into Player O4 while pivoting and assuming a good base of support for rebounding.
6. Players repeat several times and then exchange roles.

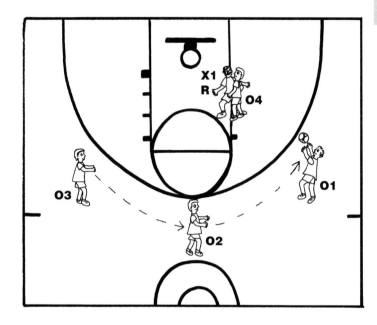

This drill provides the opportunity for shots to rebound at different angles, which makes defensive rebounding more difficult. Encourage defensive players to make contact with the players they're guarding and prevent them from going to the basket for second-chance opportunities. Caution defensive rebounders not to get caught too low near the basket. Longer shots like the ones taken in this drill have a tendency to bounce further away from the basket because of the amount of force used. If an offensive player wants to move inside the defender in a low-post position, the defender should try to move him even lower under the basket, preventing him from any rebounding opportunity.

120. Offensive Rebounding

Purpose: To develop offensive rebounding techniques.	Number of Players: 3
	Equipment: 1 basketball, 1 basket
	Time: 5 to 7 minutes

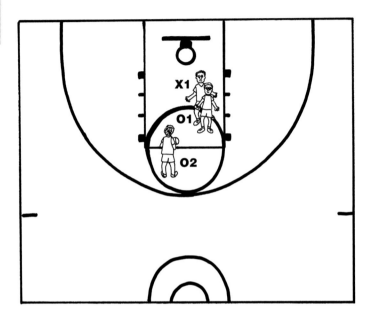

1. Position three players inside the key so that one player is standing at the foul line. The other two players, one offensive and one defensive, assume positions in the low post.
2. Player X1 starts the drill by stepping toward Player O1 while pivoting, making contact, and assuming a rebounding position.
3. Player O2 shoots the ball.
4. As Player O2 shoots, Player O1 uses combinations of rolls, reverse rolls, and swimmer's moves to gain a neutral position for rebounding.
5. Whoever gets the rebound dribbles out and becomes the next shooter.
6. Player O2, who shot the ball, becomes the new offensive post player.
7. The players repeat the action.

Strength and size are only two factors in rebounding. The ability to move quickly while rolling off block outs helps to negate size and strength advantages. Offensive rebounders can use the reverse roll (starting to roll off a block out and spinning quickly in the opposite direction) to keep defenders off balance when trying to position for rebounds.

121. Rebounding in Post Position

Purpose: To develop rebounding techniques in a gamelike action.

Number of Players: 4
Equipment: 1 basketball, 1 basket
Time: 8 to 10 minutes

1. Position Player O1 at the foul line.
2. Position Players O2, O3, and O4 in the post position.
3. To begin the action, Player O1 shoots the ball.
4. Players O1, O2, and O3 try to rebound and shoot again. If the shot is missed, play is continued until a basket is made.
5. The first player to score three baskets wins the game and becomes the new shooter.
6. Players repeat the action.

This drill allows players the opportunity to rebound and shoot while two other players are fighting them for the ball. Encourage offensive rebounders to catch the ball with two hands whenever possible and then to shoot as quickly as the opportunity presents itself, even before coming back down to the floor if possible. If they are tightly defended, offensive players should use one or more shot fakes to create a space for the shot.

122. Four-Basket Rebounding

Purpose: To develop an understanding of rebounding technique in a gamelike situation.

Number of Players: 12
Equipment: 4 basketballs, 4 baskets, 4 yellow jerseys
Time: 8 to 10 minutes

1. Position three players at each of four baskets so that Player O1 is offensive, Player X1 is defensive, and Player N, wearing a yellow jersey, is neutral.
2. On your signal, Player O1 moves away and then cuts sharply to the ball to receive a pass from Player N.
3. Player N relocates, receives a pass back from Player O1, and shoots.
4. Player X1 makes contact with Player O1 and steps toward her while pivoting and breaking down for good support.
5. Player X1 rebounds the ball, passes back to Player N, who travels as fast as she can to another basket to repeat the action.
6. Players continue action for 2 minutes and then change roles.

Player X1 provides gamelike defense in this exercise. Encourage Player X1 to watch her player as the shot is attempted, instead of the ball, so she'll be more likely to step in and make contact. Player X1 should continue this blocking-out action, with Player O1 attempting to move her away from the basket and the possibility of a rebound. If Player O1 is located near or under the basket, Player X1 should block her out and move her further under the basket.

123. Three-on-Three Rebounding

Purpose: To develop rebounding techniques in a gamelike situation.

Number of Players: 6
Equipment: 1 basketball, 1 basket, 3 red jerseys
Time: 8 to 10 minutes

1. Position three offensive players wearing red jerseys and three defensive players on one half-court.
2. You or an assistant coach stands at the top of the key with the ball.
3. On your signal, players begin moving.
4. Offensive players screen for each other to create open spaces for passes from you or your assistant. If you pass to someone, they must pass back to you.
5. You or your assistant shoot the ball as the players continue moving. Since no one is defending you, you shout "Shot" to alert players to block out.
6. After 2 minutes, reverse roles.

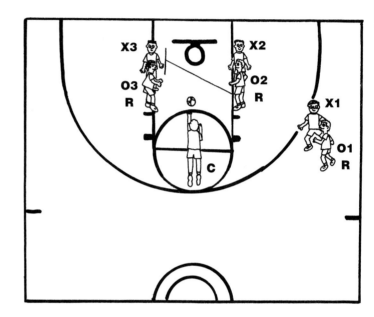

This drill provides many of the rebounding possibilities that a game offers. Offensive players moving and screening create more difficulty for defensive rebounding because defenders won't always find themselves goal-side of their player. Instead, defensive switches are called for, and players have to work over, under, and through the screens. Defensive communication can eliminate some of the confusion. Offensively, players work hard to gain advantage in positioning by executing a combination of rolls and swimmer's moves.

124. Five-Point Rebounding

Purpose: To develop rebounding techniques in a gamelike situation.

Number of Players: 6
Equipment: 1 basketball, 1 basket, 3 red jerseys
Time: 8 to 10 minutes

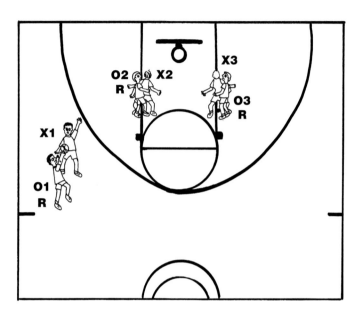

1. Position two teams of three players on one half-court. Players on one of the teams wear red jerseys.
2. On your signal, the players on the red team pass the ball to each other while being guarded by the other team. The red team must shoot the ball before the fifth pass is made. No dribbling is allowed.
3. After the shot, both teams try to rebound. The team that rebounds the ball receives 1 point and becomes the offensive team. They then inbound the ball from behind the 3-point arc.
4. If a team makes a basket, it receives the ball outside the 3-point arc but is awarded no points.
5. The first team to earn 5 points from rebounding is the winner.

If rebounding is to be valued by your players, it should be emphasized in practice and games. One way to make it important is for players to win a game using solid rebounding techniques. Encourage communication by having the defender whose player takes a shot yell out "Shot" to alert teammates to block out.

125. Vertical Jumping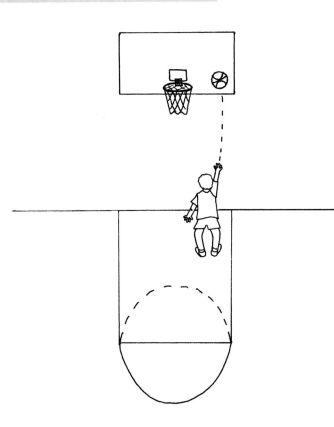

Purpose: To develop vertical jumping speed and endurance used in rebounding.	**Number of Players:** 1 **Equipment:** 1 basketball, 1 basket **Time:** 3 to 5 minutes

1. Position one player under a basket with a basketball.
2. On your signal, the player must toss the ball on the right side of the backboard and jump to tap the ball on the board using only his right hand.
3. Signal again after 30 seconds, and the player switches to the left side of the backboard using the left hand only.
4. Repeat the action.

This conditioning drill helps to develop the leg muscles responsible for vertical jumping ability. It's helpful if you and your players can keep records (mental or written) of the number of taps players make on each side of the basket to keep track of the progress made during the course of the season with this drill.

Glossary (See also the court terminology diagram on page 27.)

Back-door move: Where the offensive player fakes in one direction and then moves behind the defender toward the basket to receive a pass from a teammate.

Ball side: In terms of where ball is located on the court, it is the side of court where the ball is located; in individual defense terms, it is the side of the opponent closest to the ball.

Baseball pass: Passing the ball using a one-handed motion similar to throwing a baseball.

Big men drills: Drills designed for forwards and centers.

Block out: A rebounding position used to keep an opponent away from the ball.

Bounce pass: A pass that bounces on the floor before it is received by a teammate.

Chest pass: A pass that travels from the chest of one teammate to the chest of another.

Chicken elbow: A shooting term that describes the incorrect shooting position formed by the side extension of the elbows.

Closed space: Space that is occupied by one or more players.

Collection: The act of catching the ball.

Crossover dribble (crossovers): Moving the ball across the body from one hand to the other while dribbling.

Defensive position: The stance used when playing defense; staying low, knees bent, head up, hands active.

Double dribble: A violation in which a player either dribbles with two hands or dribbles, stops, and then dribbles again.

Drop step: A move in which the player swings one leg behind him, using his back foot like a pivot foot and opening up the legs as he changes direction.

Fast break: A play in which the team that has just gained possession of the ball moves quickly toward the basket in an attempt to get off a shot before the other team can recover and set up a defense.

Feinting: The act of changing direction quickly using various body parts to cause deception.

Forward pivot: Moving the nonpivot foot in a forward direction.

Foul line: The line on the court from which foul shots are taken.

Fronting: A defensive position where the defender is between the offensive player and the basket.

Full-court pressure: A defense used to cover the entire court.

Game marker: A rubber cone, usually about 8 inches high, used to define grid boundaries.

Game spot: A colored circle about 8 inches in diameter made of nonskid rubber. Used to define grid boundaries.

General space: The entire space on the court available to players for movement.

Get through: A defensive play where the defender who is being screened slides through a space between the screener and the player defending the screener.

Give-and-go: A play in which one player passes to a teammate, then cuts to the basket to receive a return pass for a shot attempt.

Goal-side: A position established by a player between the opponent and the basket.

Grid: A square formed by game spots or game markers used for small-sided activities.

Half-court defense: Defending an opponent after they have crossed the midcourt line.

Hand-checking: A violation in which a defender uses her hand to slow the progress of the player she is defending.

Hedge: A defensive maneuver used by a defender whose player has just set a screen. The defender steps above the screen, forcing the player for whom the screen is being set to go away from the basket.

Help-and-recover position: A defensive position used by a player not defending the ball to help the player guarding the ball. The defender moves far enough away from the player he is guarding to assist his teammate but close enough to the player he is guarding to be able to recover and prevent that player from taking a shot.

High post: An area around the 3-second lane closer to the foul line.

Jab step: An offensive maneuver in which a player in possession of the ball causes an opponent to be off balance by quickly moving the nonpivot foot forward.

J-move: An offensive move in the post area in which the player's path forms a J. Usually executed from the low-post area to the high-post area on opposite sides of the 3-second lane.

Jump stop: An offensive move in which the player jumps in the air and lands on both feet so that either foot could be used as a pivot foot.

Key: The space on the court that includes the 3-second lane and the circle where the foul line is located.

Layup: A shot taken from under the basket where the ball is played so that it strikes the square on the backboard and goes in the basket.

Low post: An area around the 3-second lane closer to the basket.

Mirroring: When the defensive player matches ("reflects") the offensive player's moves with the ball.

Off screen: The movement of an offensive player after a screen has been set on the player he is defending.

Open space: Space that is unoccupied.

Outlet pass: A pass made after a rebound by a defensive player to her teammate, generally near midcourt, to start a fast break.

Overhead pass: A pass that is executed by extending both arms over the head in a backward to forward motion.

Pass and screen away: An offensive technique in which the player with the ball passes it in one direction and moves to set a screen in the opposite direction.

Pass fake: Where an offensive player starts to make a pass, but instead holds on to the ball.

Personal space: The space that immediately surrounds a player.

Pivot: The act of turning on the front part of one foot while in possession of the ball; a movement made to increase vision or avoid defenders.

Player-to-player defense: A defensive strategy where each player is responsible for guarding a player from the opposing team.

Point: An offensive position located near the top of the key.

Post: An offensive position established in the 3-second lane. See also *high post; low post.*

Post player: An offensive player positioned in the 3-second lane; usually identified as a forward or center.

Power dribble: An offensive maneuver executed in a low-post position by slamming the ball down to the floor with both hands.

Reverse dribble: Dribbling while moving backward.

Reverse pivot: Moving the nonpivot foot backward.

Reverse roll: Faking a roll in one direction, then moving in another direction. Often used to get position for an offensive rebound.

Reverse spin: When dribbling, the player turns her back, spins, then quickly reverses and continues dribbling in the original direction.

Roll: A move in which an offensive player sets a screen, then pivots and moves to the basket.

Screening: The technique of blocking a defender's path. The offensive player calls the name of the teammate he will screen for, then moves to where his teammate's defender is. The screener blocks the path of the defender, which frees his teammate for a pass or shot. The screener must remain stationary and must not make contact with the defender.

Screen and roll: The act of blocking a defender's path by an offensive player who then pivots toward the basket to receive a pass.

Shepherding: Guiding the player with the ball in the direction the defensive player wants the ball handler to go.

Shot fake: The act of raising the arms as in a shooting motion without actually shooting, but keeping hips lowered and legs flexed.

Sliding: Extending one foot laterally and then moving the other foot in the same direction without crossing the feet.

Spin move: An offensive move where the ball handler changes directions laterally by turning his back to the defender and pivoting while continuing to dribble.

Step and clear move: A post maneuver in which a player steps toward the ball, collects it, and pivots toward the basket.

Step over: A defensive maneuver made to avoid a screen by moving the foot closest to the screener over the top of the screen.

Strong side: The side of the court where the ball is located.

Swimmer's move: A rebounding technique of moving an arm over the top of the opponent's extended arm as in a swimming motion.

Swing step: A pivoting move used to counteract a change of direction by the offensive player. To execute a swing step, the defender swings her leg backward and pivots on the opposite foot.

Switch: The act of changing defensive assignments during play.

Swoop: An offensive move used to move the ball from one side of the ball handler to the other when in a stationary position. The ball is held with both hands and moved past one knee and then the other.

Swoop-and-go: An offensive move in which the offensive player executes a shot fake, brings the ball down in a circular motion past one knee, then past the other knee, and then takes a long step past the defender.

Three-player combination: When three players are involved in an offensive play. For example, Player A sets a screen for Player B, Player B

moves off of the screen to the basket, and Player C passes to Player B for the shot.

3-point arc: A line drawn on the court 19 feet, 19 inches from the basket. It runs from the end lines on each side of the basket. A basket scored inside or on the arc counts 2 points while a basket scored from outside the arc counts 3 points.

3-second lane: The rectangular space by each basket where the sides are marked for rebounders during foul shots. The top is the foul line. It is a violation for the offensive player to remain in the lane for more than 3 seconds.

Trapping defense: A defensive strategy in which two defensive players both guard the offensive player with the ball.

Traveling: A violation in which the ball handler takes too many steps without dribbling.

Triple threat: The position of the ball that allows an offensive player a quick transition to dribble, pass, or shot.

Turnover: The act of giving up possession of the ball from one team to another without shooting.

V-cut: An offensive maneuver in which the offensive player starts in one direction with one foot, stops, and then moves in the opposite direction past a screening teammate. The path formed is similar to a V.

Visual scanning: The act of moving one's head side-to-side to gain a larger range of vision.

Weak side: The side of the court without the ball.

Wing: An offensive area located approximately where the 3-point arc and the foul line extended would meet.

Wing player: An offensive player positioned on the perimeter near an imaginary line extending from the foul line to the 3-point arc.

Zone defense: A defensive strategy in which players defend spaces or zones rather than specific players.

Index

Acknowledgments

Thanks to my friends Linda Duncan, Sharon Mitchell, and Debbie Heath for their professional expertise. Thanks to my friend Rob Bailey, whose countless hours of discussion with me about movement in sports helped generate many of the drill ideas in this book. I would like to thank all of my friends at Motion Concepts Sports Camps for helping me continue learning, and for making basketball fun for kids. Special thanks go to Ed Koss, Nick Panos, and Spike Griffith for their many, many hours working with youth and high school basketball players. To all of my players, thank you for memories that will last a lifetime.

But most of all, thank you to my sons Casey and Matthew, who will always be my MVPs.

About the Author

Jim Garland has been an elementary physical education teacher for thirty-one years. He holds a B.S. and M.S. in physical education and a doctoral degree in child and youth studies. He has coached youth and high school basketball, conducted the Motion Concepts Sports Camps since 1988, and served as a clinician on the local, state, and national level. He lives in Street, Maryland, with his sons Casey and Matthew.